Akutagawa

AN INTRODUCTION

Akutagawa

AN INTRODUCTION

Beongcheon Yu
WAYNE STATE UNIVERSITY

Wayne State University Press
Detroit, 1972

Library of Congress Cataloging in Publication Data
Yu, Beongcheon.
    Akutagawa.
    Bibliography: p. 139
    1. Akutagawa, Ryunosuke, 1892-1927.
PL801.K8Z96   895.6'3'4   75-37579
ISBN 0-8143-1467-8

To Richard C. Bedford

Contents

Preface   ix

Explanatory Note   xii

1   A Child of the *Fin de Siècle*   1

2   The Flight to Parnassus   15

3   Toward the Great Horizon   43

4   The Harvest of Death   71

5   Those Fiery Purple Sparks   109

Notes   123

Chronology   135

Akutagawa in English Translation   139

Index   143

Preface

*T*he name Akutagawa has been familiar in Japan ever since his suicide in 1927. In the West his recent fame was due perhaps to *Time*'s full-page review of Shiojiri's 1947 English translation of "Kappa," and especially to Kurosawa's *Rashomon* which won the Grand Prix at the 1951 Venice International Film Festival. However, that Akutagawa has really never lacked a small circle of Western admirers is made evident by the translations of Glenn Shaw (1930) and W. H. H. Norman (1948), among others. There are also Kojima's three-volume translations (1952–64) and more recently Will Petersen's superb bilingual edition, *A Fool's Life* (1970). Although Akutagawa is one of the most frequently translated Japanese writers (he has been translated into English, French, German, Spanish, Russian, and Esperanto), there is not, so far as I know, a single full-length critical study introducing his art to the English-reading audience. The present study, hopefully, will meet this need.

Akutagawa's career, from his meteoric appearance in 1916 to his tragic suicide in 1927, was brief and intense. He produced some 150 tales and stories which, together with his other writings, such as diaries, travelogs, reviews and criticisms, constitute nineteen volumes in the recent Iwanami edition. Protean and ever fearful of repetition, he declared that salvation lies in the full cultivation of one's potentialities—as is evident in these writings of various modes and forms—all characteristic of his dedication to art.

Some years ago Hagiwara Sakutaro, himself a poet of major stature, wrote a short but penetrating essay on Akutagawa. There are, said Hagiwara, two types of poets, the Baudelairean and the Verlainean—the one who constantly confronts critics with innumerable problems and the other who does not because of his "purity." Assigning Akutagawa to the former, Hagiwara remarked:

> Both types are to be found among Japanese writers, too. More than any other Meiji and Taisho writers, Akutagawa poses so many problems—perhaps the greatest *problem* writer who, like Baudelaire, arouses critical concern and curiosity. His writings embody those varied problems which reflect the Taisho period and its social trends, some still unresolved and likely to remain so for many years to come. To this extent his art will continue to interest readers and critics, boring none. What is most interesting is the very uncertainty of his art which receives a wide spectrum of evaluation from the highest praise to the lowest detraction.

Indeed, Akutagawa does pose a good many problems, ranging from the specific situation of the Taisho period and its literature to the general relationship of life and art; and within these extremes fall problems peculiar to Japanese literature, such as the literary and cultural impact of the West, the tradition of the short story as an art form, and the discord between formal fiction and the so-called *shishosetsu*, or "I-novel." Yet these problems, important and interesting as they are, remain subordinate to my central concern with Akutagawa's art.

Since this study addresses itself mainly to the reader not familiar with Akutagawa and his milieu, it would seem proper to clarify the scope and direction of my inquiry. The opening chapter presents the overall relationship of Akutagawa and his age; the next three chapters trace the development of his art through three stages and thereby reveal the dialectics of his mind; and the last chapter attempts to place him and his art in perspective. Such an approach, I believe, may not only lead the Western reader back to Akutagawa with greater appreciation, but also help to remove some of the prevalent biases toward him of which many Japanese critics seem guilty. (A surprising number of Japanese critics, as Mishima Yukio observed, either have concentrated on Akutagawa's personality rather than his art, or have tended to dismiss him cavalierly as *passé*.) To help bridge the critical gap between deep-rooted Japanese suspicion and continuing Western enthusiasm I conclude by suggesting that Akutagawa be reconsidered in terms of world literature.

❖　❖　❖

My text is the twenty-volume Iwanami edition of *Akutagawa Ryunosuke Zenshu* (1954–55), the last volume of which is a reader's guide prepared by the editor Nakamura Shinichiro. In preparing the present study Yoshida Seiichi's standard critical biography, *Akutagawa Ryunosuke*, and two critical collections: Fukuda Tsuneari, ed., *Akutagawa Ryunosuke Kenkyu*, and Taisho Bungaku Kenkyukai, ed., *Akutagawa Ryunosuke Kenkyu*, were particularly helpful.

For this project I am indebted to many friends; I am especially grateful to Daniel Hughes, Bernard Levine, Will Petersen, Takata Atsushi, and Carl Fernelius for their many valuable suggestions, and also to the latter for preparing the manuscript for the printer. Finally, I should like to take this opportunity to express my gratitude to the Wayne State University Faculty Research Committee whose generous grants enabled me to complete the project.

B. Y.

Explanatory Note

Throughout this study all Japanese names appear in the normal Japanese order, surname first, followed by the personal name, or the pen name that is the better known: For instance, Akutagawa Ryunosuke, instead of Ryunosuke Akutagawa; Natsume Soseki, or simply Soseki, instead of Kinnosuke Natsume; and Mori Ogai, or simply Ogai, instead of Rintaro Mori.

The titles of Akutagawa's works, like those of others, as far as possible, are given in English. All quotations from Japanese sources, unless stated otherwise, are my own translations.

1

A Child of the Fin de Siècle

*T*he beginning of the Meiji period (1868–1912) marks the birth of modern Japan when this island empire emerged from over two centuries of feudal isolation. For the Japanese it was a period of readjustment to a radically new world. Blessed with the long reign of a youthful emperor whose grand vision attracted an entourage of bold and innovative men, the Japanese overcame their insular distrust and their reluctance to look beyond their own borders. Under a national policy of modernization and westernization—terms synonymous in this instance, they launched into a three-step program to import, digest, and assimilate Western culture on a fantastic scale. Thus the Meiji period reverberated with the overall spirit of enlightenment.

On the whole, the Japanese bore well their double burden of modernization and westernization. They carved a constitutional monarchy out of Tokugawa feudalism and assumed the general façade of a modern state. Through successful wars against China and Russia, they added Formosa and Korea to their original islands, paving the way for their future imperialistic enterprise. When at last national survival was assured, it was the only instance in the Far East where other ancient kingdoms, one after another, failed in similar struggles and capitulated to the threats and enticements of Western powers.

But the burden was great, and the price was costly since Japan had to learn, if not master, in a matter of decades what had taken the West several centuries since the Renaissance to achieve. Even so, the sacrifice proved worthwhile as Taisho Japan (1912–26), now in the ranks of major world powers, took part in World War I. The spoils were varied and substantial as the Japanese invaded China, patrolled the South Pacific and Indian Oceans and the Mediterranean, and moved into Siberia. With no apparent war scars, Japan reaped a great deal and experienced a period of post-war economic and industrial boom. The people, responding to the world-wide clamor for democracy, began to make their voice heard by calling for a liberal government. There was the growing conviction that Japan had at long last "made the grade" in the arena of international affairs and was now recognized as the only Asian country capable of competing with Western powers. (When the League of Nations was formed, Japan was one of the major powers accorded a permanent council seat.) The self-confidence that arose from Japan's success in international politics was also felt in the cultural sphere. As one contemporary writer declared with pride and satisfaction: "Mentally we are now children of the world— something none of our elders could experience."[1]

For this hard-earned liberal thought to strike deep root, however, the ground was too unsettled and the time too brief. All too quickly it wilted before the threatening forces of communism, socialism, and anarchism that rose amidst domestic turmoil—economic depressions, the Great Earthquake, and subsequent social unrest. Even worse than these radical forces

2

were right-wing, ultramilitary reactionaries who destroyed the already enfeebled liberalism and gradually came to control Japan until the end of World War II.

A period of transition between the golden years of the Meiji and the dark years of the Showa, the Taisho period was thus a brief interlude, or as a historian called it, a period of "liberal twilight," the last glow of Japanese liberalism only too soon to fade before the onrushing darkness. More than any other cultural segment, literature was sensitive to this unhappy trend of history. (In Japan literary historians still must use terms, Meiji, Taisho, and Showa literature.) As though instinctively anticipating the long, deadly-sterile Showa period, Taisho literature was most self-consciously literary. Rejecting the spirit of enlightenment as a relic of the past, it eagerly embraced Western literature as its own, flirted with new trends, from idealism to naturalism, from proletarianism to decadence, and courted a multitude of movements, schools, and groups in rapid succession. Because of its feverish and ceaseless infatuations with new literary fashions, the period justly* earned the name of the *fin de siècle*, the source of almost everything modern in Japanese literature. If Taisho literature heralded modernism in Japanese literature, that was because it was nurtured, first of all, in the cradle of European *fin de siècle*. As Akutagawa reflected in 1926, the last year of the Taisho period: "The decade of the 90's, I believe, was a most artistic period. I too grew up in the artistic atmosphere of the 90's. One cannot easily escape from the shadow of such a youthful influence. This conviction only grows on me with the passage of time." And more graphically in the opening chapter, "The Era," of his autobiographical work, "The Life of a Fool," he conjured up the tenor of his generation:

It was the second floor of a bookshop. Twenty years old, he was climbing a western style ladder leaning against the shelves in search of new books—Maupassant, Baudelaire, Strindberg, Ibsen, Shaw, Tolstoy, ...
The twilight was beginning to set in, but eagerly he kept on reading the titles. What was there before him were not so

much books as the *fin de siècle* itself. Nietzsche, Verlaine, the brothers Goncourt, Dostoevsky, Hauptmann, Flaubert, ...

Struggling with the gathering darkness, he kept at their names though the books were sinking into melancholy shadow. Tired out, he was about to come down the ladder, when a bare overhead light suddenly came on. He paused at the top of the ladder, and looked down at the clerks and customers moving amidst stacks of books. They all looked singularly dwarfish and shabby.

"Life is not worth a single line of Baudelaire."

For a while, from the top of the ladder, he had been watching them.

In view of the above historian's label, "liberal twilight," Akutagawa's melancholy twilight here has a ring of prophecy and reveals the uncanny accuracy with which he captured the spirit of the Taisho period in its glory and anguish and caught the spirit of its literature to which he added a peculiar brilliance.

The Russo-Japanese War (1904–5) marked the coming-of-age of the Meiji period. This is true of its literature, especially its novel. While the romantic and other schools rose and declined, realism, earlier introduced by Tsubouchi Shoyo and Futabatei Shimei, steadily gained headway and finally developed into naturalism as the central force of the modern Japanese novel. In 1906 it came to bear perhaps its finest fruit in Shimazaki Toson's *Transgression*, which many critics hailed as the greatest novel of the Meiji period. But immediately after this, with the publication of Tayama Katai's "The Quilt" in the following year, Japanese naturalism began to move away from its European counterpart, evolving its own peculiar tradition of the *shishosetsu* that threatened to turn the entire literary scene into a wasteland.

Yet, before this occurred the scene was suddenly enlivened by the spirit of revolt—first sparked by Nagai Kafu's refreshingly romantic and exotic novels, *Tales of America* (1908) and *Tales of France* (1909), both drawn from the author's sojourn abroad. Encouraged by Mori Ogai and other literary elders, a group of young writers carried on this revolt in the direction of aestheticism. Undoubtedly the most talented of them all was young Tanizaki Junichiro, who, eliciting Kafu's praise, emerged as the hope of the new generation. Besides Tanizaki and his friends, who were mostly connected with Tokyo Imperial University, there was another group composed of Peers' School graduates, such as Mushakoji Saneatsu, Shiga Naoya, and Arishima Takeo —children of aristocratic and wealthy families. This group, named after its group magazine, *White Birch* (1910), was idealistic and humanistic. Rejecting the pessimistic, nihilistic naturalist on one hand and spurning the decadent, hedonistic aesthetic group on the other, it insisted on the moral center of all literary activites. While admiring Natsume Soseki from a distance, the White Birch group set out to find its own path.

Nevertheless, the most influential voices behind the revolt were those of the older writers, Ogai and Soseki, who, more articulate in theory than the younger writers and more forceful in their opposition to the overweening naturalists, staunchly upheld literary idealism and helped shape a new school of fiction closely after the fashion of Western fiction. Twin founders of the so-called intellectual tradition of modern Japanese literature, Ogai and Soseki evolved their position by resisting Japanese naturalism in general and the *shishosetsu* tradition in particular.

The *shishosetsu* or "I-novel" centers upon an author's private life, with events and moods recorded in a loose but intimate manner. With Katai's "The Quilt" as its early example, the *shishosetsu*, after 1910 quickly became the predominant form of Japanese naturalism and in effect the prevailing mode of the Japanese novel—to the extent that the term has since become part of common literary usage. Its continued use indicates the persistence of the *shishosetsu* tradition along with that of the *honkaku shosetsu* or the conventional formal novel. The term suggests, though perhaps vaguely, that the reality of a given novel finds its *point d'appui* in the author's personal life.

The *shishosetsu* appeared as Japanese naturalism ran its course, but without the kind of solid social, philosophical, and scientific foundations that made Western naturalism what it was—one of the most significant shaping forces in modern European literature. Without a comparable cultural framework, the modern Japanese novel developed in the direction of personal, confessional writing. And this soon aligned itself with the ancient tradition of diaries and pillowbooks and also with the native approach to all artistic activities as an effective means of spiritual and religious discipline. In stressing the primacy of natural human behavior rather than aesthetic form, the *shishosetsu* pointed to the intimacy between the artist's personal maturation and his artistic development.

The *shishosetsu* found its foremost exponent in Kume Masao. In his discussion of the *shishosetsu* and *shinkyo shosetsu* (1925), Kume, defining the former as "the kind of novel in which a writer bares himself as he is in the frankest possible manner," designated it as "the main road and quintessence of prose writing." Furthermore, the *shishosetsu*, said Kume, should properly develop into the *shinkyo shosetsu*, or the mood novel, in which the "I," once filtered, concentrated, and unified, is to register his moods faithfully. According to this view of fiction as a mode of self-expression, European realistic fiction from Balzac, Flaubert, and Tolstoy down to Dostoevsky appears to be "fictitious," altogether removed from life, and, in the last analysis, a kind of popular novel. With the meaning of the term "fiction" thus twisted and distorted, the *shishosetsu* degenerated into a kind of confessional narrative exposing the private, often scandalous side of an author's life. By regarding all fictional elements as properties of the popular novel, Japanese naturalism, though it was the first literary school to discover the rich possibilities of modern fiction in Japan, was also the first to lose sight of them.[2]

It was in direct challenge to the *shishosetsu* tradition then, that Japanese literary intellectualism under the guidance of Ogai and Soseki, both thoroughly trained in European literature (one in German and the other in English), evolved its own position. Ogai eventually turned to the genre of the historical novel, delineating the ideal human type within the feudal context; Soseki, on the other hand, attempted to present within a realistic framework a series of relentless analyses of the tragic predicament of the modern Japanese intelligentsia, and to establish the tradition of formal fiction in Japanese literature. Divergent as their ways were, both Ogai and Soseki stood on the same ground, looking forward to an objective, intellectual structure in modern Japanese literature. It was this tradition of Ogai and Soseki that a new generation of writers, particularly many Taisho writers, accepted as their point of departure. Responding even more intensely to European literature than their mentors had ever done, they were convinced that literature is also a form of intelligence, and that disciplined intelligence was what their literature needed most at the moment, the one virtue that would set their tradition in proper perspective. Such was the literary tradition Akutagawa was to carry on.

2

Ryunosuke was born on March 1, 1892 in a downtown section of Tokyo where his father, Niihara Toshizo, owned a small dairy business, not far from the foreign settlement, a symbol of new Japan. Because the hour, day, month, and year of his birth were all of the Dragon, he was named Ryunosuke signifying "dragon-child," and he seemed to become increasingly conscious of its implications. If the time of his birth predicted his future eminence, it also had an ominous side. Born to parents of supposedly "unlucky" ages, he was at once put out to nurse in keeping with the popular custom. It was a bad enough start, but even worse, his mother lost her mind within a year after his birth, and he was sent to the family of his maternal uncle to be reared mostly by an unmarried, possessive aunt. Only in 1904 was his adoption formalized, giving him the family name Akutagawa. His childhood was unhappy; he grew up, as he said later, without tasting his mother's milk, and with the secret fear that he was a child of an insane woman.

7

Akutagawa's formative period, indeed the first half of his life, was spent in his new home, in another downtown section of Tokyo where the old Edo culture was still very much alive under the long shadow of the feudal world. The Akutagawa family was old fashioned and had for generations served the shogunate in matters concerning ceremonial tea. Under the changed circumstances the family remained dilettante, indulging in the pleasures of art and refinement. In this aesthetic atmosphere he learned to love old Edo literature.

Always delicate in health, he was a sensitive and precocious boy with unlimited intellectual curiosity. Around the age of 10 he started taking lessons in English and classic Chinese, and with his classmates he founded a magazine, taking charge of editorial and other sundry chores. Meanwhile he read Bakin, Chikamatsu, and other Edo writers, some Meiji literature, and classic Chinese novels. As he said, he literally devoured a rental library in the neighborhood. Already in elementary school he seemed to anticipate the future Akutagawa, a rare embodiment of Oriental culture and Occidental knowledge, a gifted soul, yet not fit to live in this world.[3]

This initial pattern of life continued into his secondary school years. As usual, he excelled in all academic subjects, especially Chinese and history, dreaming of his future career in the latter. Reading was still his passion, with the range widening from major Meiji writers—Koyo, Kyoka, Ogai, and Soseki to European writers—Ibsen and France. Upon reaching the First Higher School, he abandoned his dream of becoming a historian and turned to literature. Although in the same class with Kikuchi Kan, Kume Masao, Matsuoka Yuzuru, and Yamamoto Yuzo, who were all later to earn reputations as writers, Akutagawa stood aloof, befriending the more scholarly Tsuneto Kiyoshi. Still an industrious student, he read Bergson and Eucken, and became enthusiastic about Baudelaire, Strindberg, France, Turgenev, and Maupassant. In a word, his literary adolescence showed nothing unconventional, nothing Bohemian, no intimations of his future career.

In his autobiographical piece, "The Youth of Daidoji Shin-suke," Akutagawa paints these early years in an altogether different color.[4] Confined to a middle-class family, he learned to resent its poverty and false respectability. The schools were no better, "gray barracks" where he endured the indignity of a prisoner. Far from being a bright-eyed model scholar, he was sickly and pale with feverish eyes and a head large and out of proportion, a student who often upset his teachers with malicious questions. Precocious, lonely, and arrogant, he stood apart from those classmates who had no intellectual ambition. His only passion was for books, to which he owed everything, and from which he learned all that he could about life.

> He did not watch passers-by in order to know life; rather he tried to understand life as it was told in books in order to watch passers-by. . . . To learn their love, hatred, and vanity he turned to books. With consuming passion he read novels and dramas that *fin de siècle* Europe produced. In their cold light he discovered the unfolding human comedy and even his soul which transcended good and evil.

To him art preceded life and nature. He was already a pessimist before he knew Schopenhauer. With his adolescent dreams of greatness shattered, he plunged into the depth of despair, and now driven by a sense of void he thought of suicide. Such is Akutagawa's somewhat incoherent self-portrait of his youth drawn near the end of his life when he became increasingly aware of his own tragic nature. Even in his youth a tragic strain apparently lurked somewhere within him.

Only after entering Tokyo Imperial University as an English major in 1913 did Akutagawa begin to consider a literary career seriously. Together with his old friends Kikuchi, Kume, Matsuoka, and Yamamoto, he twice revived *New Thought*, a little magazine which had since its founding in 1907 introduced many young writers. As he became involved with the second and third revivals of the magazine, he came to detest university lectures, cramming names, dates, and other tedious facts, such as the true identity of W. H. in Shakespeare's sonnets, and

Dickens' chronology. Writing Tsuneto Kiyoshi about this time, he declared: "I am just dying to do what pleases me."

Indeed, in his correspondence during the period 1914–15 Akutagawa divulges his youthful dreams, sorrows and ambitions. Ever torn between the opposing claims of life and art, he wonders whether or not art is the best solution to his dilemma. As a result we have Akutagawa's self-portrait perhaps not dramatic but all the more intimate. As he confides, he often feels the struggle of good and evil. Baudelaire, he says, fascinates him not so much with his hymns to evil as with his longings for good. Good and evil are but twin brothers born to the same parents, so to speak. Without such perception, all discussions of art would seem to him to be a waste of time. He has faith in art, and he feels that the bliss therefrom cannot be inferior to that of religious faith. Faith is needed not for religion alone; art, among other human endeavors, must have it. So saying, he reports joining the staff of the third *New Thought*, not because he has something special to publish but rather because he is ready to write, and "expression is man himself."

Soon he discovers how different he is from the other members of the group and believes that the most precious thing in life is to remain what he is, the way he is, however lonely it may be. Now the world is awaiting the arrival of spring. All of a sudden he has an urge to give form to something vague that stirs in his soul like grass growing out of the rain-moist soil. As he admits, he is perhaps under the spell of Nietzsche's allegory of Zarathustra. At times he despairs his lack of originality, finding all thoughts, all feelings already explored and exhausted by other artists. But even this mood doesn't last long as he yearns for love. He thrills to discover his heart beating in tune with the natural movement of winds and clouds. Within him, says Akutagawa, there seems to be a deep-seated capacity for happiness, though it usually comes only through his work.

The correspondence often reads like a series of monologues interspersed with occasional poems and dramatic fragments. There is a poem about the Milanese painter Antonio. The world has gone out of joint since the death of his master Leonardo. Some artists have taken to drinking and others are content with imitating Leonardo. Lamenting all this Antonio says:

. . . . . .

That I can never do. All I can do is to make what I believe to be my own work.

. . . . . .

Even more despairing is that my own painting, however bad, turns out to be something else, someone else's.

. . . . . .

Should this enterprise of mine fail, all my life would be a waste. Then I no longer qualify to live.

. . . . . .

Upon reading an art book Akutagawa feels that he cannot share the author's enthusiasm for Cubism and Futurism. He would gladly give credit to their theories but not to their actual works. To him Picasso remains largely incomprehensible; his favorite is rather Matisse, "a great artist," judging by the few reprints he has seen. "What I seek is this sort of art, which brims with life's vitality—the vitality of grass that grows taller and taller toward the sun. In this sense I for one couldn't accept art for art's sake. So I bid farewell to all the sentimental prose and poetry I've been writing."

Thus drawn in a direction opposite his own, as he points out, Akutagawa becomes excited over something that is "rough" and "forceful." Why, he cannot tell—except that this sort of writing makes him feel no longer lonely. The same is true of his view of art. Only recently has he begun to appreciate van Gogh, and he suspects that this is perhaps a true understanding of painting, and in fact, all arts. As he declares, "I feel like calling heretical all those arts that don't fall in line with my view. To me, therefore, most artists seem no better than hand-clever buffoons."

Early in 1915, speaking of his love that had come to a sad end, Akutagawa asks whether or not love can ever exist without egotism. Often he wonders why he must prolong his wretched existence. The idea occurs to him that suicide is man's last retaliation against God. But soon the mood changes and his will to live asserts itself. Led by Romain Rolland, he now begins to glimpse Tolstoy's great horizons. A half year later, while getting ready for his graduation thesis, he is overwhelmed by Michelangelo. Ranking him first over Rembrandt and Goya, Akutagawa writes: "All such great writers [Note his significant slip here] are singing their own songs for the benefit of mankind— at the top of their voices as loud as the trumpet at the Last Judgment. They all bring so much strength to our life. Perhaps I'm a bit genius-crazy these days."

Naturally, whenever Akutagawa and his *New Thought* group met, they discussed their own writings, encouraging and chiding each other, and castigated the naturalists, the aesthetes, and the White Birch group, three rival schools that dominated the literary scene. To these high-spirited dreamers of total conquest who took the world as their proper stage, nothing seemed to be sacrosanct, none seemed to rise to their lofty standards.

There was Tayama Katai, the leading force of the naturalist school, in whose novels they found nothing but the rhapsody of moonlight and sex. At best Katai was "a sentimental landscape painter," for most of his works consisted of travel sketches teeming with male and female devotees of Venus Libentina. He was, in Akutagawa's phrase, "free, gay, honest, and innocent as a donkey eagerly grazing on green pasture." The young generation, no matter how charitable, could not possibly take him for a naturalistic novelist, let alone a naturalistic thinker. His fame and stature they ascribed to the critical naïveté of the old generation.

Then, there was Tanizaki Junichiro, the high priest of the aesthetic school upholding the cult of *fleurs du mal*. With all his similarities to Poe and Baudelaire, however, his pursuit of the beautiful lacked their morbidity, their spiritual courage to face their own souls even if that cost them love, morality, and God. Devoid of their sense of urgency and their awareness of suffocation, Tanizaki's was merely a world of luxuriant epicurianism. His morbidity, if any, was a bit too wholesome—"much like that of a fat sultan panting under the weight of his glittering jewelry." His pursuit of sensual and sensuous beauty showed none of Poe's and Baudelaire's profundity. An incomparable master of colorful language, Tanizaki had no sense of suffering, no vision of hell which alone could make his grotesque and arabesque world of fantasy real, meaningful, and compelling.

Dissatisfied with both schools, the young artists now turned to the White Birch school. It was the time Mushakoji Saneatsu, its most forceful spokesman, was about to conquer Parnassus, ushering much needed fresh air into the stagnant literary world. With his insistence that one must remain faithful to one's self, he seemed to be a messiah to redeem the world that had long lost its true spirit in the mire of naturalism and aestheticism. Refreshing and encouraging as all this was, Akutagawa and his friends could not but regret an apparent disparity between Mushakoji the artist and Mushakoji the thinker. In their view he was too enthusiastic and impatient an artist to perfect his work. Much as he stressed the inseparability of form and content, in practice he relied on emotional appeal rather than meticulous craftsmanship.

From this it was apparent that the Japanese literary world around the middle of the second decade was eagerly awaiting a new kind of art which was electric, an art which would fuse rigorous intelligence, a sense of suffering, and perfect form, an art charged with *frisson nouveau*. And Akutagawa knew that it was his kind of art. As he wrote in "Sparks," the eighth chapter of "The Life of a Fool":

> Drenched as he was, he walked along the asphalt pavement. The rain was pouring down. Amidst the spray he smelt the rubber coat.
> Then he saw the aerial power line discharging purple sparks. He was deeply moved. In his jacket pocket he carried a manuscript to be published in the group magazine. Walking on in the rain, once again he glanced back at the power line.
> Still it was discharging brilliant sparks. Life, no matter

which way he looked, offered nothing he particularly craved. But those purple sparks, those fiery aerial sparks at least, he wished to clasp at the risk of his life.

In December 1915, at one of Soseki's celebrated Thursday gatherings Akutagawa was introduced to this foremost novelist of the day who was just entering the last year of his career. This meeting marked the beginning of their brief but memorable master-disciple relationship that joined two generations, old and new, in modern Japanese literature.

2

The Flight to Parnassus

1

*O*f Akutagawa's early writings, only a handful—translations of France and Yeats,[1] and pieces like "The Old Man" (written in 1914) and "Youths and Death" (1914)—appeared in the third *New Thought*. None of these writings attracted critical attention; nor did his more ambitious "Rashomon" (1915), which he managed to place in another little magazine. Even "The Nose" might have suffered the same fate but for Soseki's personal blessings. Upon reading this story in the first issue of the fourth *New Thought*, Soseki at once wrote a congratulatory letter to the young author: "I found your piece very interesting. Sober and serious without trying to be funny, it exudes humor, a sure sign of refined taste. Furthermore, the material is fresh and eye-catching. Your style is well-polished, admirably fitting." The elder novelist did not forget to add a word of advice: "Go on and produce twenty or thirty stories like this one. You will soon be incomparable in literary circles. 'The Nose' alone may not attract many readers. Even if it does, they may let it pass quietly. But without worrying about it, you must go on. Ignore the crowd—the best way of keeping your integrity." Through the arrangement of one of Soseki's disciples, the story was reprinted in the May issue of the influential *New Fiction*, making Akutagawa's first success all the more secure.

Set in ancient Japan, the story portrays a Buddhist priest of great renown and piety who suffers, not knowing what to do with his six-inch long nose. Although outwardly indifferent, he is much mortified, feeling that his concern about such a mundane matter does not become his priestly dignity. (He can never be a Cyrano de Bergerac who knows how to capitalize on his grotesque nose.) While searching for precedents in scripture, he subjects himself to all sorts of cures, such as boiling and stamping, and finally succeeds in shrinking his nose, but his success merely redoubles his embarrassment and shame as he now attracts even more attention. Then, much to his relief, sheer chance restores it to its original size. "Now, no one will laugh at me any more," he mutters to himself as he enjoys the breeze of an early autumn morning.

"The Nose" is based mainly on an episode about the famous long-nosed priest, found in the *Konjaku* and *Ujishui*,[2] two ancient collections of stories and tales; in psychological treatment it was inspired by Gogol's story of the same title. Yet Akutagawa's story retains nothing of the crudely simple narration and earthy humor of the original anecdote; nor does it echo the bizarre twist and sardonic laughter of the Russian writer. Sober and serious, as Soseki said, the tone is ironic, and this sense of irony derives from the author's angle of vision, the uncertainty of being human in a fickle world. The story revolves around the very attitude of the author who neither condemns nor condones. Using the human nose as a focal point Akutagawa pits his protagonist against the world and shows that neither side wins or loses completely. While his clear-eyed intelligence does not miss the slightest shade of psychological tension, his subtle comic sense contemplates human frailty with serene pity.

Already apparent in "The Nose" are three motifs: the manipulation of the absurd; the uncertainty of being human; and the morbidity of obsession. Each of these motifs is carried further in Akutagawa's later stories. The first motif is evident in "Lice" (1916), which concerns solemn-faced samurai warring over lice, and "The Dragon" (1919), in which the credulous masses gather to witness the ascent of a dragon. The second motif appears in "The Wine Worm" (1916) and "The Dream of Lusheng" (1917), both of which suggest the futility of attempting to change what one is born with, and the third in "Yam Gruel" (1916), which exposes the extremity of a human obsession fearful of its own realization.

Uniquely Akutagawa, "The Nose" refuses classification with any of the three literary schools that dominated the contemporary literary scene: naturalism, aestheticism, and idealism. Like "Rashomon," it was written in an effort to get over a recent disappointment in love, and Akutagawa meant to be pleasant and remote from reality. Fresh in conception, dexterous in execution, and cumulative in effect, the story both puzzled and delighted the reading public.

2

Although "The Nose" made Akutagawa famous virtually overnight, he was too ambitious an artist to merely indulge in his first success. His literary activities during the next few years fully indicate his ability to turn his sudden fame into something more solid and permanent. The period 1916–1919 marked in many ways perhaps the happiest years of his life, resulting in three collections of short stories, *Rashomon, Tobacco and the Devil,* and *The Puppeteer.*

The thirty-odd stories collected in these volumes are typical of Akutagawa, rich in variety and impressive in scope. In addition to conventional short stories, there are dramas, satires, fairy-tales, prose poems, and sketches—set in Japan, China, India, and imaginary lands. The Japanese stories, for instance, range from remote antiquity to the contemporary world, from the early Japanese Christian to the Edo period. Depending on his subject matter his narrative form is varied—dramatic, epistolary, allegorical, and objective—as is his style—pseudo-classical, early Christian, Chinese, and modern. Fantastic in imagery, tender in sentiment, biting in ridicule, and startling in direction, these pieces are all experimental, demonstrating the author's determination to explore and exploit different genres. Some are perhaps precious but none amateurish. Whether precocious or mature, they all attest to a high degree of literary intelligence at work.

Contemporary critics, sympathetic or hostile, quickly noted Akutagawa's intelligence and craftsmanship. One critic, designating the essence of Akutagawa's art as a combination of intelligence and humor, stressed his pose as a detached outsider observing the kaleidoscope of life. While regretting that Akutagawa's analytical power sometimes failed to go beyond common sense, the critic nonetheless lavished praise on the author's artistic integrity and his unerring sense of language. All in all, Akutagawa seemed to him to be the kind of writer who would proceed from emphasis on form to concern with content. Another critic found one of Akutagawa's central themes to be the sense of fear that inevitably follows our fulfilled expectations; he pointed out the author's capacity for perfect form, contemplation, and aesthetic distance, all of which combined to make his art unique in contemporary literature. A third critic suggested that Akutagawa's primary virtue was the purity of his aesthetic contemplation, apparent in the best of his stories, and that these stories were often almost too pure to excite the general reader long spoiled by impure works—works immature in aesthetic contemplation. Probably for this very reason his works appeared to lack in raw strength, what the critic called the throbbings of life. Despite their varied observations the critics concurred on one point: perfect form compensates for insufficient content.[3] Whatever the validity of such a verdict, it was the view generally shared by Akutagawa's contemporaries since they were prompt to label him a neo-intellectualist, neo-classicist, neo-mannerist, and the like.

Akutagawa rejected such labels designed only for the convenience of reviewers and critics because they were all too neat and simple to characterize what he was trying to do. He took every opportunity to clarify his intent: to go his own way as best he could—the only sure way of growing. In reply to the question, "Why do you write?" he said he wrote neither for money nor for the public but because something vague and chaotic within himself demanded a certain form which was at once clear and precise. Declaring that art is, first of all, expression, he challenged the general critical assumption that a writer starts with content and then frames it in some sort of form, as though there were two separate and separable processes. The common critical clichés, "stylistic obsession," "too deft" or "too dexterous," were meaningless to Akutagawa. Form, he said in effect, does not wrap content in a neat package; form lies in content, and *vice versa*. To one who cannot understand this basic truth, art will forever remain another world. Art begins and ends in deliberate expression. Write with your soul or with your life—all these gilded sermons had better be addressed to high school students. All creative activities, even those of a genius, are conscious; he is perfectly aware of what effect his single touch, his single stroke will create; if not, then he is no better than an automaton.

In Akutagawa's view, then, it would be a mistake to assume the primacy of either form or content. In the same reflections on art he in fact warned that stressing form would be equally harmful, and that in practice it might be even more harmful than stressing content, a warning apparently against a typical Japanese tendency toward the decorative or a refined preciousness. The point here is Akutagawa's passion for perfection, the quality which struck the three critics referred to above. The artist, in Akutagawa's view, must strive to perfect his work; otherwise his devotion to art amounts to nothing. For moral exaltation the reader might as well turn to sermons, but for aesthetic pleasure he must go to a work of art. And to secure this pleasure the artist must pursue his dream of perfection. It was in this vein that Akutagawa also wrote: "There is in the kingdom of art no room for the unperfected"; "A work of art, when perfected, becomes timeless"; and "In the religion of art self-reliance is the only key to salvation."

"One who has a correct view of art does not necessarily create a better work. Such a reflection makes me sad. Am I the only one in this? I pray this is not the case"—so Akutagawa wrote in "Art, etc." The truth is that Akutagawa not only had a "correct" view of art but also wrote "better" works because of it. In reference to Poe's "Philosophy of Composition" he observed that the American poet wrote his poems and stories just as a brick layer would go about his job.[4] Then turning to his own manner of writing, Akutagawa said in the preface to *Tobacco and the Devil*:

> To speak of my feelings while I am at work, it seems like growing rather than making something. Every phenomenon, human and otherwise, follows its own unique course of development in that it happens in the way it must. So as I write I proceed from point to point, from moment to moment. If I miss one step, then I am stuck. I can not go even one step further. If I force myself, something is bound to go wrong. I must always be alert. No matter how alert, it often happens that I miss it. That is my trouble.

This, according to Akutagawa, explains why a work of art in progress sometimes refuses to follow the artist's own plan, however well calculated, "just as the world may have gone out of God's hands, much as he tried to adhere to his original plans of creation." Thus, despite his insistence on conscious intelligence, Akutagawa recognized that the artist was fallible, but this human frailty was no excuse for not striving for perfection.

3

Although it is obvious that in theory and practice Akutagawa put a high premium on literary intelligence, the matter apparently was not so obvious to many of his contemporary critics who, taking the term intelligence differently, charged that with Akutagawa intelligence often degenerated into book learning and antiquarianism. The implication of their charge was that his art is all imitation, devoid of a sense of life. For example, the narrative substance of "The Nose" derived entirely from either the *Konjaku* or *Ujishui*, and for psychological analysis it followed Gogol's piece of the same title. The same is true of other stories like "Rashomon," which again relied heavily on the *Konjaku*, and "The Dragon," which in turn was based on the *Ujishui*. Likewise, both "The Wine Worm" and "The Dream of Lusheng" drew from well-known Chinese materials, and "Lice" admittedly had an oral source. Clearly, it was assumed, Akutagawa's art was bookish, and his originality, if any, was only in form, not in content. To these critics who took the terms originality and imitation in a narrow sense, Akutagawa's presumed lack of originality indicated the fatal paucity of his inner life which his art was used to camouflage.

According to Yoshida Seiichi's investigations,[5] at least sixty-two of Akutagawa's stories reveal a varying degree of indebtedness to known literary sources, Japanese, Chinese, Indian, and Western. His Western sources in particular show a wide range —the Bible, Caxton, Swift, Defoe, Goethe, Poe, Bierce, Browning, Butler, Gogol, and Dostoevsky, as well as Flaubert, Régnier, Mérimée, Loti, Strindberg, France, Synge, and others. Although Akutagawa's habit of borrowing—from mere inspiration to outright plagiarism—becomes less conspicuous as he proceeds, the proportion of borrowings to his total output of some 150 stories is very high indeed, even if one grants that such borrowing is not uncommon among writers and that reading, as a form of experience, is a very important part of any writer's life. If the practice reflected Akutagawa's omnivorous reading, it was also what made his admirer Hori Tatsuo say of him: "He finally ended without any original masterpiece. In all of his masterpieces, in every single one of them, linger the shadows of previous centuries."[6]

The question of imitation and originality could hardly have disturbed earlier Eastern and Western critics who usually showed an enviable degree of permissiveness toward such practices, over-stressing neither originality as a cardinal virtue nor imitation as a deadly sin. Even in the present century, at least in the West, we have since Joyce and Eliot, learned to accept imitation as a common phenomenon. Yet, to the modern Japanese the question still has a special significance because of their oft-alleged racial propensity to imitation, and also because of the peculiar influence of naturalists and humanists who insisted on the primacy of life over art, an attitude central to the *shishosetsu* tradition.

Akutagawa sharply disagreed with his critics on the question and affirmed the validity of literary imitation. "I am not at all ashamed to imitate the geniuses of all ages and to appropriate their crafty methods and devices." The preface to *Tobacco and the Devil* also indicates that he was fully aware of the implications of his critics' charge. It is true, writes Akutagawa, that he frequently draws from old materials with which his early education familiarized him. But it is not true that he read them with an eye to extracting possible materials for his stories. Although he does not consider such a manner of reading a serious vice, the fact is that while reading he often comes upon some interesting materials he can use later. Discovery of such materials does not insure stories since materials are just materials. As Akutagawa points out, he cannot write unless he becomes one with his material as his mind penetrates into it. And when such a union will occur, he himself cannot predict. But when it happens he knows it because his vision suddenly clears up.

From this it is apparent that Akutagawa takes reading as a major source of his literary inspirations. Especially revealing is what he has to say about the creative process, the process from reading to creation, when he describes how a story grows out of his union with a given source. "Spiderthread" (1918) may serve as an example of his personal method. The story is brief enough to be quoted in full:

1

One day in Paradise, Buddha was alone strolling around the Lotus Pond. The flowers were now in their pearly white bloom with an exquisite fragrance radiating from their golden crowns. It was morning in Paradise.

Soon Buddha paused by the edge of the pond and peered down through the lotus leaves overgrowing the water. Deep beneath the Lotus Pond lay the pit of Hell, and through the crystal-clear water the River Styx and the Mountain of Needles appeared vividly.

There at the bottom of Hell he noticed a man named Kantada writhing among his fellow sinners. Although he was a notorious robber who had committed arsons, murders, and other sins, he had done one good deed in his lifetime. Once while passing through a dense forest he came upon a tiny spider crawling along the path. Raising his foot, he was about to crush it, when he checked himself: "No, it isn't right. Tiny as it is, it must also have its life. It would be cruel of me to kill it for no good reason." So he let the creature go unharmed.

While observing Hell beneath, Buddha recalled Kantada's charitable deed to the spider and decided to rescue him out of Hell as a reward. It so happened that Buddha noticed a spider of Paradise weaving its beautiful silvery web over the saphire-colored lotus leaves near-by. Taking this spiderthread gently, he lowered it through an opening amid the pearl-white lotus flowers all the way down to the shadowy bottom of Hell.

2

In the Lake of Blood at the pit of Hell, Kantada was bobbing up and down with the other sinners. Whichever way he looked, all was dark—except for the occasional glimmer of sharp steel from the Mountain of Needles—a scene which was ghastly beyond description. Moreover, all was as still as the grave but for the faint sighs and groans rising every now and then from those wretched sinners, utterly exhausted with every known kind of infernal torture, indeed too exhausted even to cry out. The notorious robber Kantada was no exception. Choked with blood in this Lake of Blood, he was struggling in desperation like a dying frog.

Then, he happened to glance up at the sky above the Lake of Blood, and he saw the silvery spiderthread coming down from the far, faraway sky, glimmering as stealthily as if it feared the watchful eyes of the sinners. At the sight of this thread Kantada clapped his hands for joy. If he could only cling to it and climb up as far as he could, it seemed that he would surely get out of Hell. And if things were to go well, he might be able to get into Paradise. Then, he wouldn't have to be hauled up the Mountain of Needles or be cast down into the Lake of Blood.

Trembling with hope, Kantada at once grasped the thread in both hands and began to pull himself up with all his strength. Having been a great robber, he was thoroughly at home in this sort of thing.

However, Paradise rises tens of thousands of miles above Hell, too long a way for him to make it for all his eagerness. Having climbed up for a while, Kantada became so weary that he couldn't pull himself an inch farther. With nothing else to do now, he took his breath, hanging onto the thread and peering below.

His strenuous climb had been rewarded. The Lake of Blood, which he had left behind a while ago, was no longer visible in the darkness. The dreadful Mountain of Needles was only faintly glimmering way below. At this rate of ascent he might easily escape from Hell. Lacing both hands around the thread, Kantada exclaimed: "I've done it!" and laughed aloud for the first time in many years. Then suddenly he noticed right below him a myriad number of sinners climbing up and up the same thread close on his heels, diligently like a procession of ants. Kantada was stunned, his mouth agape and his eyes rolling like a dumbfounded idiot. How could this slender thread, already strained to the breaking point under his own weight, possibly sustain the crushing weight of so many? And what if the thread snaps off now? Then, he himself, after all his strenuous ascent, would be hurled back headlong into his former gloom in Hell. That would be even more frightening. While he was thus paralyzed with this prospect, hundreds and thousands of sinners kept climbing up, in a single file, along the silvery thread—after swarming out of the dismal Lake of Blood. Something had to be done at once. Otherwise, it would snap off halfway, hurling him back down to the pit of Hell.

"You damn'd sinners," Kantada shouted aloud. "This thread is mine, mine alone. Who said you could climb up? Get down, all of you get down."

At that very moment the thread snapped. All was over with Kantada. Down he plunged, whirling like a top, deep into the gloomy pit of Hell.

All that was left behind now was the faint gleam of the spiderthread hanging midair in the moonless and starless space.

3

Having seen all this through to the point at which Kantada sank to the bottom of the Lake of Blood, Buddha turned away from the edge of the Lotus Pond, and with a saddened look resumed his stroll. He must have pitied the shameless Kantada who, for his very lack of charity, was cast down to his former abode in Hell.

But those lotus flowers in Paradise seemed not at all affected by what had just happened in the world below. The pearly white flowers keep waving their calyxes around the feet of Buddha, still with their golden crowns radiating an exquisite fragrance. In Paradise it is now nearly midday.

Although even a sinner, through a small deed of charity in the past, deserves a chance to be saved, it is selfishness again that ruins him as well as others. In thesis and spirit the story is a Buddhist parable; in language and tone it is a fairy tale. As Akutagawa admitted, it required the greater care because of its brevity. Even though his lucid, elegant style suffers in translation, Akutagawa's essentially cinematic method is apparent. Masamune Hakucho missed the point when, comparing the story with *Gulliver's Travels*, he said: "Never venturing beyond common sense, it merely accepts the well-defined world of order. Granted it is meant to be a fairy tale, the author's mind too seems to indulge in the world of fairy tale."[7] Whatever this well-defined world of order, our real concern is with the source Akutagawa used for this story. For this nine out of ten readers would turn to some Buddhist source; and all ten would be surprised that it was adapted from a simple episodic parable—a thoroughly Christian one at that—in Dostoevsky's *The Brothers Karamazov*, which Akutagawa had recently read. The episode appears in "An Onion," the third chapter of Book VII, where Grushenka engages in conversation with Alyosha. The story, which Grushenka learned from her cook when she was a child, is as follows:

> Once upon a time there was a peasant woman, and a very wicked woman she was. And she died and did not leave a single good deed behind. The devils caught her and plunged her into the lake of fire. So her guardian angel stood and wondered what good deed of hers he could remember to tell to God; "she once pulled up an onion in her garden," he said, "and gave it to a beggar woman." And God answered: "You take that onion then, hold it out to her in the lake, and let her take hold and be pulled out. And if you can pull her out of the lake, let her come to Paradise, but if the onion breaks, then the woman must stay where she is." The angel ran to the woman and held out the onion to her. "Come," said he, "catch hold and I'll pull you out." And he began cautiously pulling her out. He had just pulled her right out when the other sinners in the lake, seeing how she was being drawn out, began catching hold of her so as to be pulled out with her. But she was a very wicked woman and she began kicking them. "I'm to be pulled out, not you. It's my onion, not yours." As soon as she said that, the onion broke. And the woman fell into the lake and she is burning there to this day. So the angel wept and went away. [Constance Garnett's translation]

So completely recast, "Spiderthread" as it stands leaves almost no trace of the original. By juxtaposing both versions we may sufficiently understand what Akutagawa meant by his union with the materials. Of course, he is not always so successful as in this instance. But with such a felicitous adaptation few would raise the question of imitation and originality.

4

Related closely to the question of imitation is Akutagawa's dependence on history, an early interest of his. It is his use of history as a fictional frame that led his critics to confound his intelligence with his learning and antiquarianism, and dub him a writer of historical fiction. Some forty stories, over a quarter of his total output, and all of his best pieces in the first half of his writing career fall under the category of what may loosely be called historical fiction. Akutagawa himself, in reference to "The Nose," warned against such simplistic labeling, and he was right. Today we would certainly hesitate to regard this and other stories in the same vein as historical tales.

"Rashomon" (1915), one of his earliest attempts in this genre, may help to clarify the matter. (Incidentally, the film version is actually a combination of this piece and "In a Grove" [1921].) Akutagawa's source for "Rashomon" is found again in the *Konjaku* collection. The original is a brief, simple and straightforward episode:[8] A certain rustic, having arrived in the capital to begin a career of robbery, makes his way to the great gate of Rashomon to spend the night. In this shelter he chances upon an old shrivelled woman prowling among unclaimed corpses, plucking hair for the wig market. He strips the hag and her victim and runs off. The point of the episode is the sense of fright and horror both the man and the old woman experience in their brief encounter.

Akutagawa, following his source, sets his story in the Heian period, and his narrative method here, as in "Spiderthread," is cinematic. The deserted gate of Rashomon looms in an evening storm, a symbol of the capital long deteriorating under a series of natural calamities. A man appears, a former servant who has recently been dismissed. Although armed, he is undecided whether to choose robbery or starvation. Among the scattered corpses beneath the gate he comes upon an old ape-like woman busily plucking a dead woman's hair.[9] Curious and frightened at first, he becomes indignant and demands an explanation. She tells him that she gathers hair in order to survive, and that her victim, a rapacious vendor, deserves no better treatment. As indignation gives way to desperate courage, he snatches her clothes, and leaving the old woman naked among the corpses, disappears into the darkness.

Correcting the general view that egoism is the story's central theme, one critic said: "It neither affirms nor asserts egoism. Rather in order to negate it, the author, in extreme terms, scorns and satirizes its hideousness."[10] Another critic, in the light of what he called the logic of starvation, suggested that the story expressed the anarchist position that became prevalent soon after 1910.[11] Neither critic seems really convincing, however, because both mistake the part for the whole. More likely Akutagawa tried to strike at something deeper and more basic than human egoism or the logic of starvation. And this "something" is the self that harbors those irresistible impulses of life, ultimately transcending the notions of good and evil. The theme of the story, then, is the uncertainty of the human ego which often finds itself at the mercy of those impulses whenever life asserts its primacy. The nameless characters are no better than those corpses—all completely overshadowed by the towering gate. The real protagonist is the great gate itself, which stands for the human soul impregnated with uncertain and unpredictable elements, and the atmosphere hovering over its massive structure makes "Rashomon" a powerful piece of writing. (Akutagawa felt so confident as to use it as the title story of his first collection.) More fittingly than "The Nose," "Rashomon" marks the start of his career over which it cast its long, dark shadow.

Literary historians generally agree that Mori Ogai is the founder of historical fiction in modern Japanese literature (meaning he was the first to modernize the genre), and that his legacy was further developed by Kikuchi Kan and Akutagawa. In scope, however, Akutagawa goes far beyond Kikuchi and Ogai. While the majority of Ogai's historical novels are set in Japan, in the Tokugawa period (1600–1868), Akutagawa's tales exhibit a wider range from antiquity to the modern era, and are set in Japan, Korea, China, India and 19th century Russia. His Japanese stories in particular cover virtually all the major periods, from the mythological, Heian, early Christian, and Tokugawa down to the enlightened Meiji. At one time or another Akutagawa, if we take the narrator of his autobiographical story "Cogwheels" literally, even conceived of something like an epic novel consisting of some thirty pieces arranged chronologically, from the Nara down to the Meiji period, with the people of each period as its own characteristic protagonist.

The historical novel, such as would serve to express an author's paradoxical view of life, was peculiar to the period following 1910, and the use of history for creative purposes was common to the tradition of Ogai, Kikuchi, and Akutagawa. Although Ogai's historical novels successfully created an ideal image of the feudal world of samurai, he strove to portray the past faithfully—as faithfully as contemporary realists would claim to describe their own period. To this end Ogai approached historical materials with scientific accuracy and objectivity, so that the "nature" inherent in them might unfold itself, and this refusal to alter the "nature" in history, philosophical in intention though it was, often resulted in mere documentation. By concentrating on moments of crucial significance he pursued history for its own sake, not as a backdrop for his fiction. It is this emphasis on the "nature" in history that separated Ogai from his successors in the field.

Both Kikuchi and Akutagawa were alike in turning to history as a fictional frame. Defining his kind of historical fiction Kikuchi remarked:

> In historical records there is many an incident—described in a matter-of-fact manner—which, once projected into our own subjective mind, would gain a sudden illumination as an episode of human life. In other words, if, aided by our refined modern sensibility, we retrace the past our forebears lived with little awareness, we often come across those gems of life which they let pass without notice.[12]

And what Kikuchi aimed to provide in his historical novels was a fresh interpretation of the past in the light of modern sensibility. To a large extent this seems to apply to Akutagawa too. Many of his historical tales are short, and present historical figures in new perspective often at the expense of historical convention and accuracy.

While agreeing in the main with Kikuchi's definition, Akutagawa took the term historical fiction less broadly. Although he accepted as a rule that there is no historical novel without some measure of fidelity to the general mores of a particular era, he also suggested the possibility of the kind of novel which would thematically focus on only certain unique aspects of it, say, its moral aspect. For example the Heian concept of sexual relationship differs considerably from the modern. According to Akutagawa, a writer should present this older concept in a detached manner as if he were a contemporary eyewitness and let the story produce its effect through the resulting contrast. To this category belong some of the historical novels of Mérimée and France. In Akutagawa's view there were yet no Japanese works comparable to them. Instead, there were only those that presented a glimpse of humanity common both to the ancient and to the modern. He hoped to see some young talent explore something different.

As for his own practice, Akutagawa explained the role of "a by-gone era" in his stories as a sort of fictional frame—as an equivalent of "once upon a time" or "long, long ago" of the fairy tale, and what he had to say about the matter is important to an understanding of his art.

> Let us suppose that I, seizing on a certain theme, set out to write a story. In order to give the theme great artistic power I must have an uncommon incident. Considering the uncommonness of such an incident I cannot possibly set it in modern Japan. If I do, it may only appear unnatural to the reader, and thus destroy my theme. The best way to avoid such a waste, then, would be . . . to set it in the past (rarely in the future) or somewhere outside Japan—even ancient Japan. In most of my stories I was driven by the need to avoid unnaturalness. Consequently I looked for settings in by-gone eras because, unlike the fairy tale, novelistic conventions prohibit the use of 'once upon a time' or 'long, long ago.' Once this choice of a suitable period is made, I take the next step, that is, I introduce various contemporary social conditions to make my setting appear natural. This point, that in no sense do I aim at an exact and detailed recreation of a by-gone era, I think, separates mine from the so-called historical novel.

His turning to by-gone eras, added Akutagawa, does not mean that he cherishes nostalgic longings for them. He is perfectly happy to have been born in modern Japan. True, our universal interest in things exotic may have to do with his selection of uncommon incidents, and likewise the very beauty of a by-gone era may conceivably affect his selection. While these exotic and aesthetic factors may find their way into the picture, Akutagawa emphasized that it is still the role of "long, long ago" that the past plays in his stories.

There is a group of stories executed more or less in the spirit of epic or legend, such as "The Robbers" (1917), "Heresy" (1918), "St. Christopher" (1919), "Susano-ono-mikoto" and "The Aged Susano-ono-mikoto" (both 1920). Set in the Heian, the late Heian, the early Christian, and the mythological eras respectively, these stories each conjure up those by-gone days with their peculiar atmospheres of savage flight and splendor, primitive faith and valor. The first, inspired by both the *Konjaku* and Mérimée's *Carmen*, the third, based on the Caxton version, and the last two, fashioned after the *Kojiki*, the earliest Japanese chronicle,—all have specific thematic concerns. The second story, for instance, depicts the confrontation between the native way of life and the Christian God. In the group as a whole, however, Akutagawa's thematic interest is somehow overshadowed by his exotic and aesthetic interest in the periods in which the stories are set.

There is another group of historical stories dealing with early Japanese Christians, some fifteen in all, written at various times throughout Akutagawa's career. In these Japanese Christian stories, as they might be called, theme and frame are hardly distinguishable. The subject itself was new, being one of the discoveries of the Taisho period to which contemporary scholars and artists turned with increasing fascination. Akutagawa was no exception, and he returned frequently to the newly-found materials. He was irresistibly drawn to them, no doubt, for what he called exotic and aesthetic reasons, but we cannot dismiss these Japanese Christian stories merely as the product of his alleged dilettantism. Pieces like "Tobacco and the Devil" (1916), "The Wandering Jew" (1917), and "Lucifer" (1918) couldn't possibly have been written without his antiquarian learning. Yet these and other pieces, such as "Ogata Ryosai's Memorandum" (1916), "The Martyr" (1918), and "Juliano Kichisuke" (1919), reveal something deeper and more personal than mere exoticism and aestheticism.[13]

"Ogata Ryosai's Memorandum" treats in a form of official report a village doctor's awe at the miraculous revival of a dead peasant girl by a Jesuit missionary. "Juliano Kichisuke" relates the life of a servant—the "holy idiot" whom Akutagawa loved best of all Japanese Christian martyrs—whose love for his mistress assumes the quality of religious devotion. And "The Martyr" traces the strange career of a girl who passes as a boy and is accused of fathering a child until her true identity is revealed in an attempt to rescue the child from a burning house.[14] Although few of these attain the level of his best stories, they are nevertheless significant for their themes, a variety of religious passion. Originated in the period that marked the first Japanese contact with Christianity, these materials may have served Akutagawa as he tried to reach out towards the West. Perhaps more than that, these early Japanese Christians, to him, embodied the will to transcend their frail human selves and conquer death. Their age, the 16th and 17th centuries, reminded him of the Middle Ages in Europe, a period of religious faith, miracle, and martyrdom. Akutagawa turned to this period not so much for a fictional frame as for its pervasive spiritual intensity. Or rather that was what he found in the early Japanese Christian materials.

Akutagawa's own account, quoted earlier, that he first seizes on a theme and then seeks a suitable setting for it, suggests two valuable points: the extent to which intelligence is allowed to play in his creative process, and the manner in which a theme gains clarity and intensity through its proper setting. From his declared procedure of coming upon potential materials, rather than seeking them out in old books, and since almost all of his historical stories draw from written sources, it would seem that his theme, far from being abstract, is already embedded in a germinal story or episode, and as he further develops the germinal piece the theme emerges in sharper focus.

There is still another group of stories portraying historical personages, in some of which the author's theme tends to override his other considerations. In "Saigo Takamori" (1917), for instance, he is particulary concerned to detach this recent national militaristic hero from the historical context. An elderly skeptic confounds a young historian with his thesis that Saigo, contrary to history, did not fall in the last battle of the Seinan Rebellion. The old man's sophistry in juggling actuality and probability is so persuasive that the young scholar becomes almost convinced of Saigo's survival. But the *tour de force* of the story reveals itself in the sophist's final statement:

> "I am quite satisfied to be a disciple of Pyrrho. We can never be sure about anything, even about ourselves—much less about Saigo Takamori's survival or death. Therefore, when I write a history I don't pretend to write a history free of lies. I would be perfectly content to write a history which would seem only probable and beautiful. As a young man I thought of becoming a novelist. Had I become one, I would have been writing such stories. That might have suited me better than being a historian. At any rate, I am quite satisfied to be a sceptic."

The sophist was perhaps not meant to express the author's view of history as such; even so, it suggests something of his attitude. History is regarded not simply as what happened but more broadly as what might have happened. It is certainly the artist's view of history in that it is still fluid rather than established. In this Akutagawa stands a world apart from Ogai.

What has been said amounts to this: Akutagawa uses history only as a fictional frame and is thus more concerned with its utility than its actuality. Because he uses history only to serve his artistic purposes, those who criticize his tales on the basis of historical distortion or inaccuracy go wrong. For example in his portrait of Oishiuchi Kuranosuke, the leader of the celebrated forty-seven samurai (1917),[15] Akutagawa shows no interest whatever in tracing the hero's career from the time he and his men begin plotting up to their final act of vendetta. Rather he concentrates on Oishiuchi in the aftermath of the event—at the moment he is basking in serene satisfaction while waiting for the order of harakiri that is sure to come. But his serenity is suddenly upset as he learns that his group set an unsavory pattern for vendetta-mongers, whereas others are branded as cowards or renegades for their failure to do the same. With the deeds of his group being praised for the wrong reasons, he begins to suspect that not all of his motives were pure and honorable; he even questions whether or not his feigned debaucheries resulted from selfish motives on his part. The story gives only a partial portrait of Oishiuchi, to be sure; hence the title "One Day of Oishiuchi Kuranosuke." What emerges from the series of dramatized reflections is not a shining exemplar of feudal loyalty, but an honest man with common frailties capable of self-doubt, a man of flesh and blood made all the more appealing to the modern reader. By disregarding much of the historical detail and developing the psychological conflict, Akutagawa rescues his protagonist from the myth which has long apotheosized his heroic vendetta.

In "Kesa and Morito" (1918) Akutagawa is even less concerned with actual history. Here through two dramatic monologues, we get a glimpse of the interior of the ancient lovers' minds. Awaiting the appointed time to kill Kesa's husband, Morito reflects: "I despise her. I fear her. I hate her. And yet—and yet, all this may be because I love her." On the other hand, Kesa, deciding to die in her husband's place, confesses: "I am going to die, but not for my husband. I am going to die for my own sake—yes, for having my pride hurt and my body defiled. Oh, my life has been unworthy, and so, too, will be my death." Although, according to Akutagawa, the original episode in *The Rise and Fall of the Minamoto and Taira Clans* indicates that the lovers' relationship was a sordid sexual affair, tradition has turned Kesa into a heroine who chose death for the sake of her honor.[16] When a reader protested his iconoclastic rendering, Akutagawa, referring specifically to the original version, replied that it is a sheer bourgeois myth to idolize this wretched, fallen woman as if she were some sort of superhuman paragon of chastity. In stories like these Akutagawa attempted to liberate man from all-powerful myth, and he often ran counter to tradition. When he penetrates the complex interior of humanity, history simply provides the initial frame, thus making the label "historical fiction" meaningless.

This is especially true with "In a Grove" (1921). Here again Akutagawa turns to the *Konjaku* for a usable episode but to Browning's *The Ring and the Book* for a suitable narrative mode, and he exploits his imagination to the fullest extent. (It has also been suggested that the central situation of a ravished wife came from his talk with a fellow writer.)

The story opens rather matter-of-factly with official testimonies by four witnesses: a woodcutter who chanced upon the dead body of a young samarai on a wooded hillside; a traveling priest who saw him on the road with his wife accompanying him on horseback; a constable who apprehended the murder suspect, a notorious robber; and an old woman who, identifying the slain samurai as her daughter's husband, added that the young couple was bound for their home in the country.

After these factual testimonies, the story turns sharply to another series of three mutually conflicting accounts of what really happened in the grove. As the robber defiantly admits, he did indeed slay the samurai in a duel which the ravished wife demanded with the winner to take her as his own. This version is at once contradicted by the woman's tearful confession at a temple, that she killed her husband for having witnessed her shame and then tried in vain to kill herself. But even this version turns out to be totally unreliable when the murdered husband, through a medium, reveals that his wife urged the robber to kill him, and when the robber refused he decided to take his own life.

Proceeding from the four testimonies to the three conflicting accounts of what happened, the story relentlessly develops an emotional vortex: lust, love, hate, suspicion, jealousy, anger, contempt, and resignation. It finally suggests that, as a victim of these elemental passions, man must wander hopelessly in his world of uncertainty, forever blind to the ultimate truth.

The innocuous grove becomes a symbol of life itself which is dark with human ambiguities. (It is to Kurosawa's credit that in his film he made full use of certain affinities between this story and "Rashomon.")[17] The setting is ancient, but the theme is modern, and from their peculiar combination the story draws its savage intensity.

5

There is finally a group of stories portraying famous artists as heroes. If the so-called artist stories together constitute a unique genre in modern literature, they also occupy a special place in Akutagawa's art. Being intensely conscious of his trade, he wrote more than a dozen stories about art and the artist, and most of them understandably in the early years of his career. Besides those unguardedly autobiographical reminiscences of his literary adolescence, such as "On the Seashore" (1925) and "Those Days" (1918), there are allegories satirizing critics and writers such as "Mensura Zoili" (1916) and "The Strange Island" (1923); there are also stories about works of art, such as "Noroma Puppets" (1916), "The Marshland" (1919), and *An Autumn Mountain* (1920). Some of the stories such as "Withered Fields" (1918), "The Ball" (1919), and "The Solitary Snipe" (1920), dealing with the death of Basho, the casual appearance of Pierre Loti, and the encounter of Tolstoy and Turgenev, respectively, are simple episodes. Others come to grips directly with artists at their moment of creation and here the author's theme triumphs over his historical frame.

Perhaps most typical of this series is "Creative Frenzy" (1917), a portrait of Takizawa Bakin, a great Edo novelist working on his masterpiece, *The Romance of Eight Dogs*. Based on Bakin's own diaries and written somewhat in the manner of "One Day of Oishiuchi Kuranosuke," this story was most popular among Akutagawa's friends and he himself took no little pride in it, saying that he "borrowed Bakin to write what was on his own mind."

Bakin as he appears in the story is over sixty, though with his prominent cheekbones, sturdily-set jaws, and somewhat large mouth, all suggesting his enormous vitality, he seems more like a man in his prime. Akutagawa describes in detail a typical day of Bakin's life at its peak, from his morning visit to the public bath to his lonely midnight work. Out of the massive accumulation of details gradually emerge Akutagawa's manifold themes: the conflict between the artist and his readers who are enthusiastic but remain unappreciative of his intentions; the relationship of the artist and his critics who, accusing him of imitating old masters, always lump his works with those of mediocre writers; the unsatisfactory association of the artist with his greedy, unscrupulous publishers who tempt him to prostitute his artistic integrity; the ironic relation of the artist and young aspirants who, resenting his refusal to read their manuscripts, repay him with insults and slanders; the trouble between the artist and censors who pose as the guardians of public morality and detect nothing but eroticism in his characters; and finally the sympathy between the artist and his colleagues who share his devotion to artistic pursuit.

Such a list of themes might create the impression that Akutagawa's story is merely an artist's manifesto, certainly interesting but a bit too obvious. All of these themes, no doubt, had personal implications for Akutagawa, then fresh from the first round of his literary struggle. Many contemporary readers and critics did in fact take the story as a personal manifesto. But what helps lift the story above domumentary status is the author's ability to dramatize his themes with concrete daily events and thereby create a cumulative effect. As we are led into the story we perceive with increasing clarity that it extends over three concentric circles: in the outer stand the general public which remains alien to Bakin; in the middle his family and a few fellow artists who care for him and his ideals; and in the inner, Bakin himself, alone as every artist must be when he faces his work. He is oblivious to everything else, his public, his family, and even the shared pledge with his painter-friend Watanabe

Kazan that they will go on fighting unto death. Once in this magic circle he is free of his usual frustrations and doubts. Akutagawa describes it thus:

When he finally lowered his brush to paper, some faint light was glimmering in his mind. And as he wrote ten, twenty lines, and more, the light grew larger and larger. What this was, Bakin knew from experience and kept at his writing with the greater care. Divine inspiration was in no way different from fire. Once kindled, it may go out quickly unless one knows how to feed it.

"Don't be impatient! And think deeply—as deeply as you can," Bakin kept whispering to himself, trying to restrain his brush which tended to run ahead in eagerness. What had earlier seemed to be but shattered stars, was now flowing through his mind more swiftly than a river, gaining force every moment urging him forward, whether he liked it or not.

No longer did he hear the chirping of crickets outside; nor did he have to strain his eyes in the dim light of the round paper lamp. His brush, by its own momentum, began gliding on paper without a pause. He kept on desperately as though in a mortal struggle with some supernatural power.

The stream within, like the Milky Way across the sky, came flowing from some unknown, inexhaustible source. He feared that his strength could no longer bear its torrential force. Gripping his brush firmly, he said to himself time and again: "Keep on writing to the utmost limits. If what you are writing you do not write now, you may never be able to write again."

The misty stream of light would not ebb. It swept over him, drowning everything in its dizzy rush until at last he became its helpless captive, oblivious to all, as his brush carried him along the course of the flood.

At that moment he was a sovereign whose vision transcended thoughts of gain and loss, love and hate, and whose mind remained indifferent to clamors of fame and slander. With all vanished, he was alone, experiencing only a sense of marvelous joy, a sublime ecstasy.

To this Akutagawa adds: "How could anyone alien to this heightened feeling possibly appreciate the inmost ecstasy of creative frenzy or fathom the writer's supreme spirit? In this very moment *life*, cleansed of its dregs, begins to shine before the eyes of the artist, with the brilliance of a new gem." This addition, though perhaps unnecessary, reaffirms Akutagawa's profound conviction that artistic creation is indeed a supreme human act bordering on divine mystery and that this sense of ecstasy is the highest reward any artist can hope to win.

The greatest of all of Akutagawa's artist stories, and in fact the greatest of all of his stories written during his early period is "The Hell Screen" (1918). Again drawing from old materials, this time from two different sources—one of a painter rejoicing as his house burns down and the other of a painter working on a screen depicting hell (neither episode runs to more than a dozen lines),[18] this novella portrays a tragic artist who sacrifices everything to complete his masterpiece. Incomparably better than in his Bakin story, Akutagawa here succeeds in creating an ideal artist driven by his daemon and obsessed with his dream of perfection, because here at last Akutagawa found the material that matched his gift, and both author and material achieved a rare union. It is this piece, "The Hell Screen," that elicited Masamune Hakucho's praise: "the very best of Akutagawa's stories" and "a masterpiece which gains special brilliance in post-Meiji Japanese literature."[19]

Yoshihide, or Monkey Yoshihide as he was nicknamed, is eccentric—greedy, indolent, impetuous, shameless, and above all arrogant. Odious as he is, he is a supreme artist, the greatest painter of his time. His other saving personal virtue is his passionate love for his only daughter, who is his exact opposite in every way—sweet, innocent, and obedient. Moreover, she has a quick turn of mind such as is apparent in her saving a mischievous pet monkey called Yoshihide from an impending punishment by her witty reference to the creature's nickname. After this incident the girl and the monkey become fast friends. One day the patron lord commands the artist to paint a scene of Hell on a screen. For several months he locks himself up in his studio, working on the project. As he becomes engrossed with the subject, all sorts of wild, fantastic rumors begin to spread concerning his nightmare-ridden sleep, his binding an apprentice in chains for sketches, and many other bizarre actions. Finally one day Yoshihide presents himself before the lord and reports that the picture has been competed except for the central scene featuring a magnificent carriage falling in midair. As he further explains:

> "In the carriage an exquisite court lady, in the midst of raging flames, writhes in agony, with her black hair flowing loose. Choked with the burning smoke, she turns her face up toward the roof of the carriage, with her brows tightly drawn. Perhaps her hands that grip the ripped-off screen are trying to ward off the rain of flames. And a score of ominous-looking birds flutter around the carriage, clacking their beaks. Ah, such a court lady in a flaming vehicle, I cannot paint."

With this Yoshihide makes the extraordinary request that such a carriage be burned before his very eyes, and if possible —with a young lady in it. In apparent madness that matches Yoshihide's, the lord grants the request. The appointed night arrives and everyone is invited to a deserted palace for the occasion. With the stage thus set, a carriage is drawn into the courtyard, and in it is a young lady bound in chains, exactly as Yoshihide requested. As the carriage is set afire the torches reveal that the lady is Yoshihide's daughter. The artist, horrified by the terror and death agony of his beloved daughter, is dumbfounded and cannot move to save her. Then, as the pet monkey leaps into the flames to join its mistress, an awesome change occurs in Yoshihide.

> In front of the pillar of fire Yoshihide, who was suffering infernal tortures a moment ago, stands rooted. But what a marvelous transformation! His wrinkled face now radiates a kind of blissful ecstasy as he stands, with his arms folded, oblivious to the presence of the Grand Lord. No longer does his vision reflect the image of his daughter's death agony. He seems supremely delighted with the beautiful color of the flames and the form of the woman writhing within.

It is a marked contrast to the lord's own transformation. He is now a completely changed person, pale and livid with foam gathering at his mouth, gripping his robed knees with both hands, panting like a thirsty animal. Not long after, Yoshihide completes the masterpeice which has caused so much sorrow and horror. And on the night following its completion the artist hangs himself.

All this is narrated by an eyewitness of the whole drama. Being a retainer in service of the lord, the narrator is always deferential and obsequious, consciously and unconsciously interpreting everything in favor of his master, as when he tends to gloss over the relationship between the lord and Yoshihide's daughter:

> The most prevalent rumor was that the Lord was motivated by his spurned love. But most probably he meant to punish the perversity of Yoshihide, who was so anxious to paint the Hell Screen even at the sacrifice of a court carriage and a human life. As a matter of fact, this was what I heard from his own lips.

Toward Yoshihide, on the other hand, he is uncharitable and supercilious. Because of his social prejudice and lack of perception, the narrator never understands what he observes, which only intensifies the abysmal gap between the artist and worldly authorities. To this narrative point of view the story owes much of its ambiguity, depth, complexity, and vitality.[20] Consider also the role of the pet monkey: As its nickname suggests, the creature represents Yoshihide the father. Its leap into the flames symbolizes in Yoshihide the separation of father and artist. Yoshihide the artist can now transcend his own personal tragedy, if only momentarily. The separation insures his triumph, whereas the lord suffers a complete defeat. Once within this circle of divine madness the artist, far beyond the boundary of secular power, stands alone on the lofty summit of art where he is immune and invulnerable. As a portrait of his ideal artist "The Hell Screen" marks the moment of Akutagawa's artistic triumph.

The singular intensity that pervades the novella derives

from the complete identity between the author and his hero-artist. This hero's passion for artistic perfection which becomes sheer madness is also Akutagawa's. The story evokes horror and illustrates what Akutagawa meant by the beauty of savage, naked brutality, the terms with which he attempted to define the artistic essence of the *Konjaku*.[21] It was only natural that he set the story in the same Heian period that produced the *Konjaku*. It was to his credit that in that period he discovered not only the spirit of tenderness and elegance—as many usually do, but at the same time the undercurrent of savage brutality, the quality we seldom associate with the period.

In the context of the story Yoshihide's suicide would seem to be the only logical and satisfactory solution, because it suggests the paradoxical nature of the artist who, driven by his own daemon, must transcend himself. It is this paradox inherent in his creative activities that endows his art with a sense of tragic grandeur. There is, however, something more to Yoshihide's suicide than this; because of Akutagawa's unmistakable identity with his hero, we are tempted, as Akutagawa himself was in his last days, to see Yoshihide's suicide in the light of his own. While, as Miyamoto Kenji pointed out, Akutagawa the artist has his hero experience an artistic triumph, Akutagawa the man cannot leave him forever in that sublime ecstasy; and his own later suicide, like his hero's, is what results inevitably from the very conflict within himself between the artist and the man.[22] In this sense Akutagawa was never an artist for art's sake, a writer content to remain in his enchanted circle.

3

Toward the Great Horizon

1

The first period of Akutagawa's career was one of glory and splendor that reminded his contemporaries of Pegasus' flight to the sacred Parnassus. Ever eager to explore new fields of the imagination, afire with passion for perfection, and driven by fear of repetition, he wrote some seventy stories, a little less than half of his total output, in a span of three years or so. But what may have seemed Pegasus' flight was actually a strenuous uphill climb, a conscious revolt against the contemporary literary world.

Armed with the conviction that every literary revolt, even when against oneself, deserves sympathy, Akutagawa carried out his revolt in two ways. First, he opposed the tradition of the *shishosetsu* which, subordinating art to life, had in effect caused their confusion. Rejecting this cult of life he upheld the autonomy, the superiority, of art. Second, he opposed the three major schools which divided the contemporary literary scene. Acutely aware of the dark forces in human nature, he could not accept the idealist position that free cultivation of individuality would automatically lead to a better world; painfully sensitive to life's suffering, he could not partake of the sensual orgy of the aesthetic school, however alluring; and deeply committed to rigorous intellectual discipline, he could not share the naturalist capitulation to the lawlessness of human instincts.[1] While criticizing each of these schools Akutagawa nevertheless sought to harmonize their ideals in his own kind of art.

If his emphasis on perfect intellectual control was what made his conquest of Parnassus possible, it also made him experience a peculiar sense of loneliness. As Akutagawa said:

> As we strive toward artistic perfection, there is something that stands in our way. Is it possibly our indolence? No, nothing of the sort. It is of stronger nature—difficult to define. It is like what grips the heart of a man who, the higher he climbs the mountain, feels the more nostalgic toward the world below the clouds. Whoever cannot understand what this means, must remain a stranger forever as far as I am concerned.

Perhaps this sense of isolation, this yearning for the world was also present when Akutagawa declared: "I am an artist for art's sake, and at the same time I am not. Life is too vast." Most certainly, it was his instinctual love of life which in a moment of frenzy he had disdained as not being worth a single line of Baudelaire, and from which he had turned to books in emulating his early literary master France. (Indeed, he took special note of Renoir's advice: If you want to learn painting, go to museums.) There was also his increasing self-doubt as to whether or not in his dedication to artistic perfection, he had somewhere been led astray from the path of his own being which demanded a total, not partial, fulfillment for its own survival. This danger of transcending life, or rather of bypassing life, Akutagawa had already expressed in "The Holy Man"

(1915) and "The Wine Worm" (1916), and was now expressing in "Tu Tzuch'un" (1920)—all with one recurring theme: You cannot help being what you are: and living honestly as a human being is the best way you can be faithful to your destiny.

While scaling his Parnassus, Akutagawa no doubt remembered his youthful dreams of "great horizons." Now standing on the lonely summit and gazing at the great horizon unfolding far below and beyond, he wondered whether or not he had really achieved something that would make him equal to those great masters who seemed to have succeeded eminently in harmonizing art and life, a harmony which enriched both. As he again heard the nostalgic call of life, his doubts about himself —his life and art—inevitably darkened his vision.

Self-doubt resulted in artistic impasse which occurred soon after "The Hell Screen" (completed in April 1918). As if he had instinctively sensed this impasse, Akutagawa turned away from the short story to the novel. In the next year or so he tried the latter form twice in "Heresy" (November 1918) and "On the Road" (July 1919)—the one set in his favorite Heian period, dealing with the early confrontation between the native way of life and the Christian (featuring as hero a son of that Grand Lord of "The Hell Screen"), and the other set in the contemporary period depicting the world of young Japanese intellectuals. Neither was completed, however, and he tended to blame his publishers. He felt that he could write a novel if only they would forget, and let him forget, his reputation as a short story writer. Yet, he may have suspected that the novel, the conventional novel form, suited him least. For this reason perhaps, speaking later of the unfinished "Heresy," he declared, in effect, that the artist's mind, like a mountain stream, could not turn back.

In the meantime Akutagawa kept writing short stories. Following "Heresy" he turned out "Mr. Mori," "Those Days" (both in December 1918), and other pieces, set in the contemporary world. In April 1919 he wrote two pieces, "The Marshland" and "The Dragon." The former portrayed a painter who lost his mind because he was unable to create the kind of work he dreamed of, a pathetic contrast to that willful genius Yoshi-hide. The latter portrayed a vindictive monk who, by duping people to believe that a dragon would rise from a lake, avenged himself on those who ridiculed his big nose. "The Dragon," which in conception and execution is an imitation of his earlier pieces, "The Nose," "Lice," and "Yam Gruel," indicates that Akutagawa had reached the point where all he could do was repeat himself. Of "The Dragon" he wrote several months later: "In the realm of art there is no such thing as pause. 'No prog-ress' means regress. When an artist regresses, there always be-gins a sort of automatism; that is, he turns out the same kind of stuff. Once this automatism sets in, the artist is clearly on the verge of death. When I wrote 'The Dragon' I faced such an ar-tistic death."

Artistic death, in Akutagawa's case, signified his crisis as a man. Since the trouble stemmed from his deliberate aliena-tion from life, and life alone could offer a satisfactory solution, if he was to survive as an artist, the only alternative was to re-turn to it. Apparently in a hopeful mood and in spite of failing health Akutagawa, at the request of the *Osaka Mainichi*, under-took a four-month visit to China. His account of this visit, how-ever, showed no tangible signs that the journey helped him. At this point a trip to Europe might have been more helpful —an idea his friends suggested but his family turned down in fear that it might aggravate his undermined health. A leisurely journey through his literary homelands, as his old friend Tsu-neto Kiyoshi pointed out, might have had a salutary effect on his creative career and his inner life, and forestalled his later suicide.[2] He remained at home, however, and had to fight his way through this crisis without whatever benefit a journey to Europe might have afforded him. Thus began his descent from Parnassus.

2

This descent, as was always the case with Akutagawa, be-gan as a matter of personal necessity. It marked his middle period, and coincided, significantly, with the critical moment of the Taisho period.

After 1916 a series of profound changes occurred in the national scene. The unprecedented prosperity which World War I had brought to Japan did not last long. Following the war the country plunged into serious economic depressions, accompanied by increasing unemployment. In 1921 trade slipped to two-thirds that of 1919. The Great Earthquake of 1923, which shook the populous Kanto area, accelerated this deterioration. As small industrial and financial institutions were absorbed by gigantic monopolies, Japan moved into a rapidly advancing capitalist economy.

Under the pacifist banners now unfurling in the wake of the war which had sought a permanent peace, the once pervasive democratic trend, in response to the Bolshevik Revolution of 1917, turned toward socialism. With labor and farmers movements spreading across the nation, the old slogan, "for the people," changed to a new one, "for workers," and the Japanese intelligentsia also began showing interest in social problems. The first May Day in the history of the Japanese labor movement was observed in 1920. The Socialist Alliance was organized, resolving the conflict between anarchism and socialism, and heading further toward the formation of a proletarian party as its political arm. To solidify the movement's intellectual front the official organ, *Seedsman*, appeared in 1921, providing a variety of proletarian theories of literature and art.

With the Great Earthquake the proletarian literary movement seemed to suffer a temporary setback as the alarmed government authorities began tightening control over leftist activities. But the Diet, under mounting popular pressure, finally passed a manhood suffrage bill in 1925, though simultaneously enacting a bill to increase the powers of the police to deal with "dangerous thoughts." Leftists, now favoring legal political action, came to form the Social Democratic Party and the Farmer-Labor Party in 1926. Left-wing writers, recovering their force, organized the Proletarian Writers Federation in 1925.

The literary scene, meanwhile, was taken over by neo-sensualism supported by its own magazine, *The Literary Era*, which first appeared in 1924. The new school, no doubt reactionary in the eyes of leftist writers, reflected the general mood of despair hovering over the debris of the earthquake. Much like the Dadaist movement which rose from the ruins of the war in Europe, this school aimed primarily at replacing neo-intellectualism with its own logic of the senses thereby dispelling the boredom of life. Affirming the coming advent of a proletarian society, the neo-sensualists also accepted as a matter of course the eventual disintegration of their own social class. In advocating a sort of hedonistic nihilism they went further than their predecessors.[3]

Although World War I, which ushered the West into a new century, also had a far-reaching impact on Japan, it was the Great Earthquake that shattered Taisho intellectuals more immediately and profoundly. To them, this earthquake, which ruined the heart of Tokyo, signified no mere natural calamity; to them it came as a social and cultural cataclysm heralding the imminence of a universal doom—a Japanese version of the Lisbon earthquake of 1755 that shook the entire continent of Europe. To them, Kikuchi Kan seemed to be a true prophet of the hour when he declared: "In an emergency such as this earthquake, art is useless, to say the least. Our recent experience only helped expose the ultimate futility of all artistic endeavors."

In the midst of such emotional outbursts Akutagawa remained aloof, apparently less perturbed than most of his contemporaries. While conceding that his friend Kikuchi's oracular declaration might apply on the conscious level of artistic activities, he suggested that it would certainly not affect art as an expression of our unconscious impulses deeply rooted in life. Art, he argued, may be superfluous to life, but it is the kind of superfluity that makes man what he is. Therefore, we must strive to create such superfluities if we are to maintain our human dignity. "I passed through the Marunouchi ruins," Akutagawa said. "What I saw there, however, was something that even great conflagrations could not possibly destroy." To him it was inconceivable that an earthquake, being a natural calamity, could change a writer's view of life as such. Its impact on literature, he thought, might make itself felt in two opposing trends, the one exploiting raw human emotions and the other searching for inner excitement. The former, according to Akutagawa, would result in one kind of fiction catering to the many, and the latter in another kind appealing to the few. And surely both trends would soon gain momentum.

Akutagawa was accurate in thus noting the sudden eminence of both popular literature and neo-sensualism in the wake of the Great Earthquake. Even earlier, speaking of the popular fiction that appeared in 1920, Akutagawa had in fact defined its function as a needed channel between society and literature, and hoped that the new kind of writing would gather force as a more serious trend. At the same time he was equally charitable toward neo-sensualism, despite his reservations. True to his conviction that every literary revolt deserves sympathy, he regarded the development of the latter school as inevitable and hoped that critical hostility would not deter it from becoming a meaningful literary movement.

From this it is not difficult to anticipate Akutagawa's favorable response to proletarian literature. After all, he viewed socialism as "not a matter of right or wrong but a matter of necessity." In reply to a magazine questionnaire on this point he wrote in 1923: "First, from my point of view of society, life, and art, the so-called proletarian literature ought to exist; and second, since it ought to exist, there is no reason to oppose it." Literature is not unrelated to politics; it is in fact one of the major characteristics of literature, Akutagawa points out. The paths to the summit of Parnassus, like the streets of Tokyo, are not made to order for the gratification of the followers of art for art's sake. His only hope is that proletarian literature will not lose its freedom of spirit, namely the critical spirit which can discern egoism in its foes as well as in its friends. Or as he reiterates elsewhere, we cannot wholly transcend our time; nor can our souls remain unmarked by our social class. There are, as he takes it, three kinds of proletarian literature. The first he defines very generally as simply that which thrives in a proletarian culture; the second is propagandistic in support of the proletarian cause; and the third, even if not communistic or anarchistic, is based on what he calls the proletarian soul. If there is to be any new literature in the future, Akutagawa believes, it will be this third type, "the poetry of life," which becomes a reality only through the artist's perfected craftsmanship. Akutagawa's interest in and support of proletarian literature were due both to his sensitivity to his time and to his personal conviction. His insistence on critical intelligence, poetic spirit, and technical mastery shows that his support was sincere and not simply a frightened intellectual's feeble gesture toward the onrushing tide of his time. With fresh enthusiasm he greeted the new trend mainly because it also seemed to open toward what he called the great horizon. In "Hero," Chapter 33 of "The Life of a Fool," he wrote of this period:

> From a window of Voltaire's house he looked up at a lofty mountain. Over the summit of the glacier-hung peak there was not even the shadow of a vulture to be seen. But a stubby Russian tenaciously kept climbing the mountain path.
> After the night fell over Voltaire's house, under a bright lamp he composed a tendency poem, recalling the Russian who had pursued that mountain path:
> The greatest follower of the Decalogue,
> You broke it more than anyone else.
> The greatest lover of the people,
> You despised them more than anyone else.
> The most consuming idealist,
> You knew reality better than anyone else.
> You are a flower-scented electric locomotive
> Our East produced.

Art is the creation of a lonely man, an artist on his solitary quest. Convinced of this, Akutagawa never allowed even proletarian literature, much less neo-sensualism, to lead him astray from his new path toward the great horizon.

As a leading writer of his generation Akutagawa was much sought after, and his middle period 1920–1924, was as eventful as the first had been. Although troubled in spirit by his dark self-doubt, he made the journey to China, went on a lecture tour, and fulfilled various other obligations. After his Chinese visit his health steadily deteriorated. The Great Earthquake and family affairs further aggravated his condition. Yet he would not relent in his professional activities. At the request of publishers he edited two anthologies of English and contemporary Japanese literature. He also brought out two collections of his own critical writings. On top of it all he produced four volumes of short stories. Although some of these warranted his fear of repetition, many suggested how furiously he was revolting against his earlier work and how determinedly he was striking out in new directions. There were few areas or genres he left untried.

First, nursery and fairy tales: Earlier Akutagawa had already written such flawless pieces as "Spiderthread." Now he followed them up with "The Dog and the Flute" (1918), "Tu Tzuch'un" (1920), and "The Holy Idiot" (1922), set in Japanese antiquity, ancient China, and feudal Japan respectively. Although the Chinese story prompted Masamune Hakucho to repeat his old charge that the author merely indulged in a world of complacent melodrama,[4] taken together the stories indicate Akutagawa's ability to adapt himself to the peculiar demands of the genre without sacrificing his identity. For example, "The Three Treasures" (1922) is a playlet of three scenes concerning a young prince's attempt to rescue a fair princess from a rival suitor. From three robbers the prince purchases a pair of boots, a cloak, and a sword—all claimed to possess magical power. Although it soon becomes apparent that he has been duped, the undaunted prince challenges his rival, a black king, who, provided with three genuine treasures, can win the princess' hand. But the young prince's courage impresses him, and realizing his own wrong, they become reconciled—a happy ending which is consistent with the pattern of the genre. A personal meaning suddenly emerges, however, when the black king points out that he is not a devil, and that a devil-like black king exists only in fairy tales, and the prince in turn addresses himself to the audience:

"Our dear audience. We've at last awakened. The devil-like black king and the prince with his three treasures exist only in fairy tales. Awakened, we cannot remain in this fairyland forever. Look, beyond this mist the world is vast. Let us step out of this never-never land of roses and fountains. Let us march into that new world—a wider world, uglier perhaps, yet a more beautiful and larger fairyland. Whether that world awaits us with joys or sorrows, no one can tell. All we know is this: We'll march as bravely as a file of soldiers toward that world."

As it has often been, "The Three Treasures" can be read as a personal allegory in that the prince's larger world suggests the author's new sense of challenge.

Steeped in the tradition of Swift, Voltaire, France, and Shaw, Akutagawa also had an ability to adapt even fairy tales to his satirical purposes. Seizing on a favorite story of Japanese children about a war between the monkeys and the crabs, he turned it into a story of the class struggle between the have's and the have-not's. In his version, ironically, the victorious leader of the crabs dies leaving his surviving family in misery: his wife degenerates into a prostitute; their first son becomes the head clerk of a brokerage firm; their second son turns into a love-crazy novelist; and their last son becomes an arrant fool like his father. While "The Monkey-Crab War" (1923) prefigures the dark future of the class struggle, "Momotaro" (1924) is a savage indictment of Japan and the Japanese. The original, another favorite of Japanese children, follows the heroic career of Momotaro from his birth in a peach (hence his name Peach-Boy) to his conquest of the neighboring island of ogres. On this expedition he is assisted by three faithful followers: a dog, a monkey, and a pheasant. In offering his own version Akutagawa may have had in mind a certain Chinese statesman (he had met such a person during his Chinese visit) who said he hated the Japanese idolatry of this hero conqueror. If, then, the ogres here are taken to be the pacifistic Chinese, Momotaro represents the Japanese whose imperialism has been encouraged by three major groups: the war-mongering military establishment; the profit-minded businessmen; and the fame-loving intellectuals. Although the story apparently raised no outcry in 1924, in the Showa period, the heyday of Japanese expansion over the Far East, a satire like this would have been impossible to publish.[5]

A dream motif or a dream voyage also served Akutagawa's satiric purposes. Earlier in "Mensura Zoili" (1916) he had used this form to describe a land of Aristophanesean frog people who apply their measuring machine exclusively to literary works from abroad—a satire aimed at the double standard of Japanese critics. Now in "The Strange Island" (1923) he adopted the same motif to further emphasize his point. While reading *Gulliver's Travels* the narrator falls asleep, and in his dream he is guided by an old man through an island piled with a mountain of vegetables left over from market. Despite the surplus the undaunted inhabitants frantically continue to produce all varieties while only the blind, crippled, and disabled serve as official inspectors. Ironically, the vegetables sell briskly regardless of how these inspectors judge them. The old guide turns out to be Gulliver himself and then quickly transforms into the narrator's nephew who arrives with a magazine editor's request for a manuscript. Here Akutagawa pokes fun at the fashion-mad, chameleon-like Japanese literary scene in general and ill-qualified critics in particular.

Akutagawa's interest in the early Japanese Christians still continued in several stories written during this period. In them, however, we no longer detect either the beauty of martyrdom or the reality of miracle which religious faith alone can inspire. Instead, many of them dramatize religious conflict, a theme which inevitably asserts itself once placed in its proper historical and cultural context. As early as 1917 Akutagawa, in a planned trilogy, had hoped to tackle the confrontation between the native and the foreign gods. "The Smile of Gods" (1921) reads like a partial realization of this project. The cultural theme gains dramatic force as Padre Organtino, in his fantasy, witnesses the native gods congregating for the dawn of history, and gradually learns from the genius of the land about the mysterious force that has successfully transformed all foreign ideas into its own. "Ogin" (1922) relates the recantation of a Christian family at the stake. A couple recants their new faith for their adopted daughter Maria Ogin, who in the last moment hopes to join her real Buddhist parents even in Hell. They all go free, as the narrator adds, "perhaps the most shameful incident in the chronicles of Japanese Christian martyrs." This conflict between the native and the Christian faith appears again in "Oshino" (1923). A samurai's widow begs a padre to save her only son from a mysterious illness. In his zeal he graphically narrates the life of Christ with his last words: "My God, my God, why hast thou forsaken me?" Much to the padre's astonishment, this only turns her away. She declares that he who serves such a cowardly master has no right to touch the son of a brave warrior.

In this connection it is well to mention Akutagawa's stories set in the early Meiji years, the very first period of cultural contact between modern Japan and the West. "The Ball" (1919) is presented as the reminiscence of an old lady who, as a young girl, danced with an exotic French naval officer at a ball and while still remaining ignorant that her partner was none other than Pierre Loti, remembers only his words: "I'm thinking of those fireworks—fireworks like our lives." What Akutagawa tries to present here is not so much a cultural contrast as a poetic evocation of the so-called Rokumeikan era—gay, fresh, and dreaming of a brave new world. But there is no such lyric nostalgia in "Otomi's Virginity" (1922), set in the last days of Edo under siege. On returning to the deserted house to retrieve her mistress' cat, the maid Otomi must face a young beggar. She is willing to forego her honor in exchange for the cat. The story depicts an aspect of feudal morality in the changing context of history. Set in the same early Meiji, "The Dolls" (1923) recreates a now impoverished family which must sell their treasured dolls to a foreigner. In revealing the pathos of those caught in transition from the old to the new it is a Chekhovian piece.[6]

"The Tangerines" (1919) is perhaps the most Chekhovian of all of Akutagawa's stories. More properly, it is a sketch or an episode. One gray wintry evening the narrator boards a Tokyo-bound train. Just before the train pulls out a peasant girl hurries in and sits opposite him. As the train roars through a tunnel, he suddenly realizes that everything around him—the evening paper filled with mundane gossip and the plain-looking girl passenger—is but a symbol of life which is incomprehensible, banal, and boring. When the train rushes out of the darkness the girl pushes a window up and tosses a half dozen tangerines among three shouting boys at a railroad crossing. These tangerines, deeply colored in the warm evening sun, falling over the children bring the narrator a moment of revelation. The young girl, it dawns on him, is probably going to Tokyo to work as a maid, the boys are her brothers waving and shouting their good-byes to their departing big sister, and the tangerines are meant to be her surprise reward to them. "At that moment I was able to forget my gnawing sense of fatigue and ennui, and even this absurd, banal and boring life itself." It is a moment of epiphany, an incident Akutagawa personally witnessed, so moving that he later related it to his friend Kikuchi Kan. The piece appeared together with "The Marshland" under the title "Some Incidents I Encountered," and, significantly, in the same month as did "The Dragon," which seemed to Akutagawa to signal his artistic death.

Written in a similar vein are "The Flatcar" (1922) and "The Lilies" (incomplete, 1922), based this time on the experiences of an acquaintance. Both purport to be a young proofreader's childhood reminiscences and are touched with nostalgic beauty. "The Flatcar" is a particularly delicate story. An eight-year old boy, Ryohei, hoping for a ride on a flatcar, goes out every day to a railroad construction site outside his village. One afternoon he finally gets his chance. After a long exciting ride he and the crew arrive at a terminal, and there he is told they won't return to the village for the night. Frightened and bewildered, he sets out for home alone, repressing his tears and running along the railroad tracks until he reaches the gate of his house. "This incident often comes back to his mind for no obvious reason. For no obvious reason. Tired as he is, even now as then he can see stretched in a thin broken line that road with dusky groves and hills." Some readers may prefer the story without such an addition, but they may change their mind as it becomes clear that the incident, growing into a symbol of life, suddenly relates itself to the present. Simple and unassuming as it may seem at first, the story is structured with care. The tone of these sketches is deliberately subdued, and perhaps for this reason they all touch us with a singularly tender pathos.

4

Speaking of "Autumn" (1920), one critic called it an important work in which Akutagawa for the first time turned to objective realism.[7] In this the critic is quite right, but to reach this point Akutagawa had to come a long way. Even while completing "The Hell Screen" he had expressed his dislike of its "bombastic" tone and said that, being already in the thick of it he would pull through anyway. Then, leaving "Heresy" incomplete, he had turned more and more to the contemporary scene, as "Mr. Mori" (1918) and "On the Road" (1919) suggest. The former is presented as a friend's encounter with his old high school English teacher who, long after retirement, by sheer habit must go on teaching—a portrait of this half-pathetic, half-Quixotic character. Admitting that the material was somewhat different from that of his earlier stories, Akutagawa had hoped to remain free of the various labels tacked onto his art. "On the Road," originally entitled "The Morning," discards a narrative frame altogether. A novel of adolescence reminiscent of Soseki's *Sanshiro* (1908) and Ogai's *Youth* (1910), this piece recreates the world of university students—much more sophisticated in many ways than those of the older generation. Torn between idealistic and cynical views of love, the protagonist seeks to define his own view. The task was apparently too great for him, and the conflict is left unresolved. Akutagawa himself was not satisfied with the way the story had turned out, which may account for his leaving it incomplete, though he said he had learned from his failure. In all likelihood he lacked that which would sustain him through a novel-length story; moreover, without his customary narrative frame he found it difficult to work on contemporary material. In a word he was not yet ready to write a realistic story that did not employ an elaborate fictional frame.

By the time he wrote "Autumn" Akutagawa must have felt he was ready and in fact did succeed in getting directly to his material. At first he still felt far from certain, having been "not used to this sort of thing." But finding that it turned out better than he had feared, he said that it wasn't bad at all. And a little later he confided with some measure of satisfaction that he had overcome at least one difficulty.

In the story, Nobuko, a literary-minded girl, loves her cousin who also has literary ambitions, but she gives him up for the sake of her younger sister, and leaves Tokyo to marry another man. As she adjusts to her practical husband her old dreams also dissipate. Then she visits her sister married to the cousin who has by now established himself as a promising writer. Quickly realizing that she is intruding into her sister's love nest, Nobuko leaves with a quiet pang of loneliness. Originally entitled "The Season of Resignation," this story follows the heroine's changing moods which culminate in a serene despair. There is nothing in the story that suggests the familiar intensity of Akutagawa; there is instead a subtlety with which he probes into the heroine's mind. One evening during her visit she goes out in the yard with her brother-in-law, and they peep into the hen-house. He whispers: "Sleeping," to which she adds a mental comment: "Yes, with her egg stolen." The author's eye misses nothing and his hand is sure and steady, keeping the whole story from lapsing into sentimentalism. "Autumn" led Mishima Yukio to say, in effect: A work of gray monotone which, innocent of Akutagawa's usual wit and mannerism, does not bore us. In this direction there seemed to lie a wide field most suitable for him. He should have written more such non-masterpieces as this.[8]

"Oritsu and Her Children" (1920), which came out a few months later, is equally realistic in detailing the last days of a dying mother surrounded by her three children: a married daughter not her own, a son from her previous marriage, and another by her present husband. Earlier, in his story of the dying Basho, "Withered Fields" (1918), Akutagawa had dealt with a similar situation but used the poet's own diary and the reader's historical associations as his frame of reference. Now, without such a pre-existent frame, he had to create in a domestic setting all the shades of reaction the three children would show toward their dying mother. He managed their highly complicated situation with considerable skill, though Yoshida Seiichi complained that the author wasted too much attention on his setting and left his characters flat without a gripping sense of sorrow.[9] Akutagawa had initially thought of having the daughter describe the wake and funeral, but the story, in the present version, ends precisely with the mother's death—seen mostly through her younger son's eyes. The story remains an *étude*, so to speak, pointing to "The House of Genkaku," one of the author's last pieces. To get to that point he had to write two more stories in a similar vein, "The Garden" and "A Clod of Soil."

The central focus of "The Garden" (1922) is the formal garden of the Nakamura estate which, with its miniature mountains, ponds, streams, and pavilions, serves as a mirror reflecting the fate of this once-influential family caught in the ravages of history. As the older generation disappears quietly with the deaths of the old couple, their three sons each must suffer the havoc which time works on man and nature. The first son dies of consumption, the second leaves for a career of debauchery, and the third remains indifferent to whatever befalls his family. Ten years later, the second son returns home to die. In the face of approaching death he sets out to restore the now devastated garden, helped by his little nephew, son of his deceased brother, who is to carry on the family tradition. When the task is completed he becomes ill and dies, apparently with some sense of fulfillment. But all is gone. Where the house once stood with its splendid garden, there is a railroad station. The only survivor to remember the history of the place is the little nephew, now a struggling young art student, who often in moments of exhaustion hears the voice of that dying man: "When you were only a child you helped me. Now, please let me help you."

"The Garden" is admittedly based in part on the childhood of the author's painter-friend Oana Ryuichi. The last section, however, goes beyond this fictional frame to present the young artist as the representative of the third generation of a family who completes a cycle of family history. The perceptive delineation of the sense of fulfillment that man experiences in his apparently futile struggle against nature and history, led Uno Koji to call "The Garden" one of the best stories written during Akutagawa's middle and later period.[10] Miyamoto Kenji concurred with this view and pointed out that the ailing man's obsessive vision of the garden was even more compelling than the painter's in "The Hell Screen." With specific reference to the scene describing the second son at work—uncertain of details but always sure of his phantom vision—Miyamoto remarked that in the story, which marked the peak of Akutagawa's aestheticism, the author might have glimpsed the fate of his own art.[11] What resulted from the dying man's last restoration is particulary significant:

Even so, when autumn arrived, the garden stood out from the dense shrubs and trees. True, there was no longer the *Sei-kaku-ken* nor the waterfall to be seen, as in the old days. In fact, there were no traces of the former elegance once created by a celebrated landscape gardener. But still *the garden* was there. The water of the pond, once again limpid, mirrored the round miniature mountains; and once again the pine trees serenely spread out their branches in front of the *Senshintei.*

As this and the last scene suggest, "The Garden" is not wholly a story of dark despair; man is still capable of a sense of achievement in his struggle with death.

"A Clod of Soil" (1923), which poignantly sketches the simple pathos of endurance, compassion, and loneliness, impressed Kataoka Teppei, among others, as the ultimate of Akutagawa's realism.[12] The source of this story was presumably provided by the same person that had helped Akutagawa with "The Flatcar," but "A Clod of Soil" as it now stands has little to suggest that. Depicting a peasant family it is written in simple language befitting the central character, Osumi, and moves straight toward the climax.

When her son dies after long confinement, Osumi feels hopeless, not knowing how to face the future alone with her daughter-in-law and little grandson. It appears the only way to survive is to have her daughter-in-law, Otami, marry the deceased's cousin, but this secret hope comes to nothing as the young widow is determined to carry on a man's work for the sake of her son's future. Relieved of her initial fear of being left alone, Osumi is grateful and gladly takes charge of all household chores. As time goes on, however, she becomes doubtful of this arrangement as Otami continues to expand their land holdings. With all her attempts to curb the daughter-in-law's acquisitive mania proving useless, she realizes that whatever she may try, she will enjoy neither leisure nor relaxation until her last day. In the ensuing years she becomes a veritable work horse always panting under a mountain-load of chores. In the meantime Otami, now her merciless taskmaster, parades as a living model of filial piety. Then, the very day the district authorities are to confer an official citation on her, Otami suddenly dies of typhoid. The burial is concluded with a shower of condolences, and that night Osumi is alone, freed from all fears and assured of relative comfort. But what she must face in her loneliness seems worse than her years of drudgery, worse than all of her previous fears put together. As the story ends:

> Osumi opened her eyes in surprise. Her grandson was sound asleep next to her with his innocent face upturned. As she gazed at his unaffected face she suddenly realized that she was a wretched creature; and that at the same time her son, Nitaro, and his wife, Otami, whom fate bound up with herself, were also to be pitied. This change of mood at once washed away all of the hatred and anger that had accumulated over these nine years; it also washed away whatever future comfort she had been looking forward to. The parent and her children, all three, were wretched; and she, now the only one to survive, was the most wretched of them all. "Otami, why did you die?" she whispered, in spite of herself, to the newly departed. Suddenly tears began to stream down her cheeks.
>
> Only after the clock struck four did Osumi fall asleep in exhaustion. And the chill day was already dawning over her thatched roof.

Akutagawa is intent on exposing the tension between Otami as she is caught up in the mania for work, and Osumi who endures like her slave. He traces the course of fate which drives the one to death and the other to loneliness, and eventually both to a clod of soil. What finally emerges from this apparently hopeless predicament is the enduring peasant soul which refuses to yield in its pathetic struggle with fate. Here for the first time Akutagawa succeeded in making visible something akin to what he called the proletarian soul, which he both adored and dreaded. When Masamune Hakucho's enthusiastic review appeared, Akutagawa at once expressed his gratitude and added that the review had brought him the greatest joy since Soseki's congratulations on "The Nose."[13] What hope, what stake he personally rested on this piece is not difficult to surmise.

When Akutagawa turned to the contemporary scene, producing these satiric pieces, personal sketches, and realistic stories, critics hailed them as indications of a significant shift in his career. Moreover, when over the same period he also published a group of autobiographical stories, such as the Yasukichi series and "The Youth of Daidoji Shinsuke," they all agreed that the author had at last come round to confessing his life in the manner of the *shishosetsu* which he had long opposed.

In response to the general clamor—Write more about your own life; confess more boldly—Akutagawa once replied that he had been doing that all along, his stories being more or less the confessions of his own experiences. If, he said, he refuses to make himself a protagonist and write unabashedly about the incidents and events that happen to him, it is because he finds it distasteful to tell all merely to gratify curiosity-mongers and by these means to court fame and fortune. Suppose, Akutagawa continued, he writes about his sexual experience. Readers will be excited; critics will congratulate him for taking a new direction; and friends will decide that he is at long last revealing himself completely. Mere thought of it would cause him to shudder. Even Strindberg wouldn't have condescended to publish his *Confession of a Fool* had he had enough money; and when he decided to go ahead with it, he wouldn't have it appear in his own language. What he will do if he should lose his following, Akutagawa admitted, he doesn't know. But right now he is not that hard pressed; he can still manage to make a living. Thus, sickly as he is, Akutagawa's mind is sound and normal with no symptoms of masochism. Hence his refusal to write a confessional novel.

Akutagawa's refusal arose from personal distaste. What, then, was his considered view of the *shishosetsu*? In his friend Kume Masao's theory of the genre Akutagawa noted two points of importance: that a *shishosetsu* must be a novel, not a mere record of life; and that, first person narrative or no, it must always have "I" as its protagonist. So far so good. The real issue, in his opinion, was Kume's assertion that the *shishosetsu* is the main road of prose literature. According to Kume, the *shishosetsu* differs from what European critics call the *Ich Roman*. Whether in the first, second, or third person, it is a novel about the author's real life, though it is no mere autobiography. To cite specific examples: Rousseau's *Confessions* is a mere autobiography, whereas Strindberg's *Confession of a Fool* is an autobiographical novel, that is, a novel. Akutagawa, however, could see no substantive difference between the two, not to mention the supposed difference between an autobiography or confessions and an autobiographical or confessional novel. If, said Akutagawa, there is any difference it is simply a matter of labeling, as in all literary classifications; and at most it refers only to a quantitative difference. What makes a piece a *shishosetsu* is that it is autobiographical, and therefore such a novel insists on something "not fabricated," which amounts to denying the writer's freedom, the very base of all artistic activities. As long as art abandons freedom, it degenerates into a tool of propaganda, philosophical and political. This sort of "honesty," Akutagawa stated, is not the main road to art. On the contrary, the main road of art exists only in masterpieces, or in the summits they represent. For that matter he could not take Uno Koji's argument seriously that the *shishosetsu* is more congenial to the Japanese than the regular novel. As he reiterated, his objection was not to actual *shishosetsu* but really to the doctrine of the *shishosetsu*. Akutagawa wrote the Yasukichi series and "The Youth of Daidoji Shinsuke," not because he espoused the doctrine of the *shishosetsu*, but rather because at this stage he had both the need and the desire to write about himself as an act of self-confrontation.

The Yasukichi series, written over a period of three or four years (1922–25), consists of ten stories: "The Fishermen's Market," "From Yasukichi's Notebook," "The Greeting," "A Young Mother," "A Certain Love Story," "The Hack Writer," "Cold Weather," "The Boy," "The Ten *Yen* Bill," and "The Early

Spring." ("From Yasukichi's Notebook," in turn, is composed of five, and "The Boy" of six smaller pieces.) In this series of third person narratives Yasukichi makes his first appearance, a very inconspicuous one, in "The Fishermen's Market," an episodic sketch, and makes his exit with the last story in a similar manner as he listens to an account of his friend's love affair. In the intervening stories he does play the title role, so to speak, passing himself off as an English teacher at the Naval Engineering College, and in two or three places he unmasks himself as a writer. All the stories suggest that Akutagawa was experimenting with his personal experiences at the time, with only a vague notion of scope and direction.[14]

The first critical reaction when the series began to appear was that the author failed in his apparent attempt to write autobiographical stories. Discussing specifically "From Yasukichi's Notebook," "Cold Weather," and "The Boy," a panel of reviewers generally agreed that, neither natural nor straightforward, he still had too much of the poseur. They all wished that these pieces had been written as sketches. As an example they referred to the ending of "Bowwow," the first piece of "From Yasukichi's Notebook." One day Yasukichi chances to observe a paymaster insisting that a beggar-boy bark if he wants to receive an orange. A few days later, when Yasukichi goes to the office to pick up his pay he is kept waiting. Rather than letting the officer say "In a second," Yasukichi ventures his rehearsed line: "Sir, shall I bark?" His voice as he said it was "gentler than the voice of an angel." The panel members felt that he shouldn't have said "Sir, shall I bark?" or he should have done so only mentally. To contrive such a forced ending was, in their opinion, typical of Akutagawa.[15] Apparently the panel judged these stories by their pre-conceived standards of the *shishosetsu*, and neither they nor other critics were impressed by the series. Masamune Hakucho, for example, admitted that "From Yasukichi's Notebook" was more revealing of the author's true personality than any document of his personal life, but flatly stated that the series on the whole was artistically inferior.[16]

The Yasukichi series, it is true, is not particularly impressive; yet, unengaging as it is, there is something that can be said for its suggestiveness—especially in the light of the works that followed. In addition to Akutagawa's usual artistry, there is a delicate freshness in some of the stories. (Shiga Naoya, for instance, found "The Greeting" refreshing.)[17] There is considerable variety; there is quiet irony often mixed with humor; and there is also a kind of eeriness which prefigures some of his last pieces—as in a passage describing a lizard changing into a streak of fuel oil; a dialogue between black caterpillars (both in "From Yasukichi's Notebook"); the suggestion of an imagined cosmic chill shrouding the earth (in "Cold Weather"); and the episode of a wet nurse quizzing a four-year-old protagonist about the parallel cart tracks of a deserted road (in "The Boy").

After finishing "From Yasukichi's Notebook," Akutagawa wrote to one of his former colleagues at the college, expressing his hope to go on to portray some of their mutual friends from days which he remembered fondly.

> In any case, recollections of my school teacher days are not unpleasant. (Yet even in dreams I am dismayed to find myself still teaching. Maybe, memories are unreliable. Or maybe it's good to have these unreliable memories.) To a young man of 25 or so, life could be pleasant, and he should be grateful for these pleasant dreams. . . . Nowadays I often inject some extra oil to lubricate life, and when I realize I've overdone I hasten to sprinkle sand over it.

As the letter suggests, the pleasant memories cast a sort of faint melancholy over the series. Although the series presumably covers the author's period of teaching at the Naval Engineering College (December 1916–March 1919), nowhere does Yasukichi resemble Akutagawa as a soaring Pegasus over the literary scene. What emerges instead from these third person narratives is a young man who plays with the tricks of fiction writing and much to his chagrin finds himself more successful as a hack writer of an obituary than as an artist. At best he is sensitive, observant, and mildly vocal about his view of life, but certainly shows no intense drives. Because of his essential passivity he does not qualify even as an anti-hero. As a result the series is no better than Kikuchi Kan's "Keikichi" series and Tokuda Shusei's "Toru" series, to both of which it has often been compared.[18] It is a series of disparate portraits of the young man as an artist rather than a single portrait,[19] and Akutagawa was probably no happier with it than were his critics. He let Yasukichi make a quick exit and attempted something different. The result was "The Youth of Daidoji Shinsuke" (December 1925), a series tracing the growth of an artist. As the subtitle, "A Certain Mental Landscape," indicates, it is a more unified portrait of the artist as a young man and thus stands in sharp contrast to the Yasukichi series.

"Daidoji Shinsuke was born in the neighborhood of the Ekoin Temple of Honjo. As far as he could remember, there was not one single beautiful street, not one single beautiful house. Particularly his own house. . . ." Despite the drabness of his birthplace, Shinsuke enshrined it deep in his heart; he came to love nature that was languishing in the midst of an old, decaying civilization. One morning as he visited the river front with his father the usual anglers were not there. He then sighted a dead body with close-cut hair floating over the rippling current among the briny, weed-entangled pickets, a scene which was to continue to haunt him (I. "Honjo"). Shinsuke grew up without tasting his mother's milk. He drank only bottled milk delivered from the dairy every morning. It was a shameful secret, a life-long secret he wouldn't share with others. Soon he learned to prize it as he thought of Romulus raised on wolf's milk, and felt something almost human in the eyes of a white cow staring at him over the pasture fence (II. "Milk"). He suffered the shame of a destitute middle class family which had to parade with airs of respectability; above all, he was ashamed of his own father, a small, bald-headed man in retirement. His sense of guilt was born out of this secret shame (III. "Poverty"). Superior student that he was, he knew he was never well-liked, a boy with an inordinately large head and a pair of glittering eyes. The gray barracks-like school reminded him of Dostoevsky's *The House of the Dead* (IV. "Schools"). The only company he sought in his loneliness was an endless list of books from which he learned about life, his own soul, and the beauty of women and nature. This process of going "from books to reality" always served him as the sole way to truth (V. "Books"). Shinsuke could not form friendships with his classmates without measuring their intelligence. Those without intellectual ambition remained strangers. Morbidly class-conscious, he felt at home only with his own kind, pitying those beneath and hating those above (VI. "Friends").

Here ends "The Youth of Daidoji Shinsuke." In the post-script Akutagawa said he feared that the present installment would not do justice to the title, and hoped to add three or four more in the future. Because "Daidoji" seemed so promising, many critics regretted its incompleteness. When it was published, a panel of reviewers concurred that the piece was different from and in fact better than the Yasukichi series.[20] Kume Masao, a member of the panel, said: "Not naked yet. It is an Akutagawa in clothes, if not in his usual full dress or in his favorite gray monkish robe. At least a casually dressed Akutagawa." Kume still stood by his doctrine of the *shishosetsu*. Another panel member, Kubota Mantaro, was more to the point: "A very moving piece of writing. The author is right in his subject. He was used to standing outside with a casual glance or rather with such a pose as to conceal his furtive stare. In this piece, though, he holds firm and steadies his eyes."

"The Youth of Daidoji Shinsuke," even in its incomplete form, excels the Yasukichi series, but still fails to dramatize the latent tension between man and artist. What it creates is a kind of personal tension between the feudal and the modern, the poetic and the intellectual, which would eventually shape one into an artist. "Daidoji Shinsuke" had to be left unfinished because the author, possibly due to his ill-calculated strategy, was unable to dramatize his nostalgia as a more basic tension, the

tension between life and art. As is apparent in two chapter fragments, "Void" and "Pessimism," he struggled unsuccessfully to
continue "The Youth of Daidoji Shinsuke."

These two additional chapters were written sometime in
1925. With a Faustian will to be "great," Shinsuke ventured in
three directions: First, he turned to philosophy and studied
Bergson, Eucken, Lamettrie, Spinoza, Kant, and the like. Except for Nietzsche and Schopenhauer, none satisfied him. His
failure in this direction, he soon came to realize, resulted from
his insufficient background, his lack of sustaining energy, and
his obsession with the senses. Second, he ventured into literature, but much as he tried to express the various shades of emo-
tion, all he could manage was a series of exclamations. Then he
tried to express things exactly as he saw them only to discover
his artistic impotence. Last of all he turned to translation: he
decided to translate Poe not so much for linguistic exercise as
to learn the secret of his art, but the result was a failure. From
all this he learned one bitter lesson—he had no talent. In his despair he thought of suicide for the first time in his life. His tragedy, as Akutagawa scribbled in English on the margin of his
manuscript, was the tragedy of "endeavouring to be great and
finding to be small" ("Void"). Shinsuke was already a pessimist long before reading such famed pessimists as Schopenhauer and Weininger, though his pessimism, being non-theoret-
ical, had little to do with their kind of philosophical abstraction.
If he devoured Schopenhauer, that was because in the German
philosopher's aphorisms he hoped to find weapons with which
to defend his own pessimism. But again the weapons were only
weapons. "The blame he laid on life—He remembered an ever-
dim lamp light, his own 'Confessions,' and the dead body with
close-cut hair floating over the river he had seen at the briny
dawn. But what continued to cause anxiety to this twenty year
old Shinsuke. . . ." As is obvious in this disordered, often falter-
ing, and incomplete ending of the second fragment, "Pessimism," Akutagawa simply could not go any further in his renewed attempt to continue "The Youth of Daidoji Shinsuke."

In his first struggle to justify his existence Akutagawa found only the tragic despair that resulted from "endeavouring to be great and finding to be small."[21] He was yet too young, however, and too obsessed with his dreams of greatness to accept this despair as inevitable.

4

The Harvest of Death

1

*T*his deliberate attempt to reach "the great horizon," whatever it added to his art, was in Akutagawa's opinion a virtual failure. The intensity of "The Youth of Daidoji Shinsuke" derived largely from this sense of failure which as an artist he refused to accept, while trying to justify his worth in the throes of death. In the last two years of his career Akutagawa, as he confessed, lived with thoughts of death. That this was no exaggeration is all too plain from what we know of his several suicide attempts, though each time his will to live asserted itself. Earlier he had written in "The Maxims of a Midget":

Life is like an Olympic meet sponsored by a madman. We must learn how to wrestle with it as we go along. Those who find it an absurd affair, had better walk out at once, suicide being one of the exits. Whoever wishes to stay on, however, must go on fighting, not minding his wounds.

And in "Dialogue in Darkness," one of his posthumously published writings, he hoped to make a fresh start:

Akutagawa Ryunosuke! Akutagawa Ryunosuke! Put your roots down deep and firm. You are a reed blowing in the wind. The weather may change at any time. Just stand your ground. That's for your own good. And also for your children's. Don't be conceited. Don't be servile, either. You are going to make a fresh start now.

Some of his correspondence during the period also concerns this struggle between life and death that occupied Akutagawa's mind. Writing to an ailing friend early in 1925, Akutagawa complained of the trouble he himself had with his stomach, intestines, and nerves, and added: "Although I don't think living is any fun, I don't think death is any fun, either. I'll try to live as long as I can. So you too try to live even one day longer." A year later he reported the same physical deterioration and his planned visit to a spa for rest. Late in 1926, writing from Kugenuma, he hoped to consult a psychiatrist during his next visit to Tokyo. A month later he confided that an old woman in the street suddenly turned into his dead mother. Now it seemed to him that the anguish of nerves was the worst of all. "We humans don't get crushed by one thing alone. When, however, a countless number of things accumulated over the years come crushing on us all at once (though you may dismiss all this as a sort of neurosis), it becomes really intolerable." He was amazed he could still write while all these things were going on. On the same day he wrote to his psychiatrist-friend that even a "No Trespassing" sign often made him feel his way blocked. This mental disorder, said Akutagawa, was perhaps caused by his physical deterioration, but he had every reason to be "jumpy" about it in view of his mother's insanity. A few days later he described his life of dependence on constant medication—opium extracts, enema, and veronal.

A ghost from the other world—that was the way Akutagawa appeared at this time, according to his friend Uno Koji, who called on him in Kugenuma toward the end of 1926:

> His long abundant hair all dried up without its usual luster; his arched eyebrow under which his sharp eyes became triangular now and then; his large and thick mouth; his sunken, hollow cheeks; and his long, pale, angular face—all made him not of this world. As I looked at his face I felt a chill passing through my frame.[1]

As ill luck would have it, in January 1927 his brother-in-law lost his house in a fire and committed suicide as he was suspected of arson. All the consequences, including heavy debts, fell squarely on Akutagawa's shoulders. A man of *giri* or rather a victim of what the Japanese would call a sense of obligation, he wrote: "Misfortune has befallen my relatives. Helpless. Right now I am running around to straighten things up." A fortnight later he again wrote: "Many problems, many troubles, and many worries in my hands." And it was in the thick of all this he wrote resignedly: "In my next life I wish to be born into a grain of sand."

In the seas of trouble and under the shadow of death, writing was the only form of existence available to Akutagawa. All his writings during the period are pervaded by an odor of death; some read as though written by Death's own hand. "After Death" (September 1925) is an unpleasant story. In a drugged dream the narrator-hero returns home from death only to learn that his wife is married to a man below her station. Upon waking he intensely regrets his selfishness.[2] "One Day of the Year's End" (December 1925) is an episode with symbolic overtones. Again it begins with a dream in which the narrator walks along the edge of a precipice overlooking a marsh where two snowy waterfowl swim. Waking up he takes an acquaintance to a cemetery where they locate Soseki's grave after a long search. On his way home he sees a cleaning man from a placenta disposal company struggling to pull his cart up a slope and decides to help him with the hope of gaining relief from his depression by mustering his remaining strength. "The north wind from time to time swept straight down the long hill. As it did there was a rustle among the bare trees in the cemetery. Experiencing a peculiar sense of excitement in the twilight hour, I kept on pushing the cart frantically as if wrestling with myself." Akutagawa, by his own account, rewrote this apparently simple piece many times until he hit on the idea of the placenta cart. This, together with the initial dream and the visit to his beloved mentor's grave, impregnates the little episode with a heightened sense of pathos.[3] The last paragraph especially makes one wonder if it was meant to symbolize the author's strenuous efforts to create some of his last masterpieces, such as "The House of Genkaku," "Kappa," and "Cogwheels."

In "The Records of the Dead" (September 1926) the author reminisces about the death toll in his family: mother, sister, and father. "My mother was insane and to her I've never felt filial intimacy." This insane mother died in tears, and his father died in a manner no better, exclaiming: "Now here comes a battleship decked with flags. I want all of you to shout *banzai!*" For some reason the author feels affinities with the sister who died just before he was born. "As if in a fantasy I often feel a middle-aged woman, somewhat like mother and somewhat like this sister, is watching over me from somewhere." On one of his rare visits to their graves he wonders who was perhaps the happiest of the three. The tone of the piece is that of one who knows he is soon to join them beyond the grave. This sense of close intimacy with the dead was probably what impressed Shigo Naoya.[4] Grateful to a friend for objecting to Tokuda Shusei's criticism that it is not a story, Akutagawa commented: "I myself don't think it is so bad a piece."[5] Then, there is "Three Windows" (June 1927), the last of Akutagawa's stories published before his death. A battleship now out of service is lying in dry dock and it can hear its own cracking. Painfully aware of its own uselessness, it is haunted with memories of its long seafaring career checkered with victories and defeats.

This 20,000 ton battleship in the white dry dock raised its high bow proudly. Right before it, many frigates and cruisers were arriving and departing. There were also some new submarines and hydroplanes. The sight of them only made the battleship feel a sense of mutability. Watching over the Yokosuka Naval Base under the changing weather, it was quietly waiting for its fate to be sealed. All the while it was somewhat uneasy about the way the decks were warping steadily.

All we have to do is to put Akutagawa in place of the battleship class A.

In "Defeat," the last chapter of "The Life of a Fool," Akutagawa wrote: "His hand holding the pen started shaking. He started drooling. His head had never once cleared up except when he woke from the slumber induced by 0.8 gram of veronal. Even then, it lasted only a half hour or an hour. In that twilight he had lived from day to day, resting as it were on a slender sword with the edge broken." The description was true only poetically, however. As his correspondence suggests, the last several months were in fact the most productive period since his early years. He was always busy writing. The nearer his final hour approached the more frantically he wrote. In a letter to his friend Saito Mokichi, a psychiatrist-poet, Akutagawa likened himself to the medieval royalist Kusunoki Masashige fighting his last battle, and concluded: "All I want now is animal energy, and then animal energy—and then animal energy." Gathering all that was left to him—strength, intelligence, and imagination, he was resolved to erect a monument that would outlast death. In this he succeeded, as is obvious in his last writings: "Literary, Too Literary," "The House of Genkaku," "The Mirage," "Kappa," "Cogwheels," "The Life of a Fool," and "Man of the West"—rich in variety, tragic in tone, and inimitable in expression; in short, uniquely Akutagawa. By embracing death he turned defeat into triumph.

2

Some fifteen years after Akutagawa's death, Furuya Tsunatake, evaluating his critical writings as a whole, found them trivial in quality and devoid of any sense of reality. Superb craftsman and brilliant intellectual that he was, Akutagawa the critic showed few signs of maturity in other respects, a striking contrast to the contemporary naturalist and idealist writers. For Furuya, those very qualities which made Akutagawa's art appear so intellectual, refreshing and unique in the eyes of his contemporaries turned out to be fatal weaknesses.[6] Here, however, Furuya seems to combine the two critical principles, of partial and total negation, which Akutagawa once denounced through the mouth of Mephistopheles. The principle of total negation is to deny the artistic merits of a given work by its very merits; to condemn, for instance, a tragedy for its terror and pity or for its lack of felicity and gaiety. Since this procedure is too patently biased, Mephistopheles urges the alternative principle of partial negation: This work is written intelligently, to be sure. But that's all there is to it.

What Akutagawa chides through Mephistopheles is the cowardice of contemporary critics playing safe for the sake of expediency, as well as the half-heartedness of fellow-artists taking up criticism as a hobby. Unlike them, he firmly believed that criticism as an act of self-expression is indisputably a form of art. If art is immortal, then criticism is also immortal, for man will forever ask: What is art? Criticism is thus a response to this most basic question. Yet Akutagawa was too much of an artist to suggest the separation of art and criticism. Criticism or critical appreciation, as he took it, is really an act of collaboration between artist and critic in that the latter attempts his own creation on a given work of art as his subject. (This is one of the themes of his story *"An Autumn Mountain"* [1920].) Akutagawa wholeheartedly subscribed to Baudelaire's statement that every poet has a critic within himself, if not always *vice versa*. "A genuine critic," said Akutagawa,

> will take up his critical pen to sift rice from husks. More often than not I too experience such a messianic urge within me. Most of the time I take up criticism for my own sake— in order to sing myself intellectually. Thus criticism, as I understand it, in no way differs from writing novels and haiku.

As an act of self-expression criticism is a form of art. With this conviction Akutagawa took criticism as part of his artistic activity, always eager to discuss his own trade, write reviews and prefaces, and ponder the problems of art and criticism. With the artist and the critic within himself challenging each other, he produced a great deal—enough to be collected in three volumes. By virtue of his intelligence, insight, erudition, and passion, much of his criticism is still worth reading, especially in connection with his creative writing.

A short story writer who would rather be called a poet,[7] Akutagawa wrote much about poetry and poets. He himself wrote poetry of various forms, traditional and modern. His interest and competence in haiku especially was a fact widely recognized by his contemporaries. A genuine lover of haiku, he was, as one critic observed, the only Taisho writer since Soseki who achieved any degree of distinction in this genre.[8] Unlike Soseki, who preferred Buson, Akutagawa turned to the earlier tradition of Basho. The first thing that impressed him was no doubt Basho's complete mastery of this seventeen syllable form of poetry, but then he learned to find a great deal more in the poet. The lengthy notes on Basho which he wrote over the years attest to the nature of his very personal interest in this poet.

What is it he finds in Basho? First of all, it is the poet's intense and unremitting dedication to his art which can best be compared with that of a swordsman facing his supreme test of life or death. As is suggested in Basho's dictum, "If one can write but several excellent pieces in his lifetime, he is a poet; and if he can write ten of the same quality, he is a master," the way of haiku, for Basho, was not just a leisurely pastime. In him Akutagawa discovers a daemonic poet who could not remain a recluse. He also admires the poet's awareness of impermanence which never lapsed into sentimentalism. He valiantly walked his way without flinching. Thus as a man too, Basho, says Akutagawa, was truly heroic, an aspect which has not been properly appreciated. Then, there was Basho's boast that the benefit of haiku is a rectification of common language.

77

Basho meant by this, Akutagawa explains, not a correction of grammatical errors but giving a soul to common language because he sensed its potentialities as poetic language. In the same spirit he used classical diction, Japanese and Chinese, with the result that his poetic vocabulary was enormously enriched, ranging from archaic to modern, from foreign to native. In this regard Basho may share the title of bard with Whitman, as Akutagawa points out.

The brevity of haiku leaves little room for music, and excessive concern with music is contrary to the true spirit of haiku. Yet if one remains indifferent to the beauty of its music, he will miss half of its poetic effect. What was remarkable about Basho, Akutagawa believes, was that he seldom neglected this musical element in haiku. The same with Basho's use of auditory and visual imagery; in this he excelled Buson and other later haiku masters. There was also something else, Akutagawa points out, namely a sense of ghostliness or diablerie in Basho's poetry, a sign that he was part of his time.

But there are two more points to which Akutagawa returns with special emphasis: Basho's indebtedness to Chinese literature and his awareness of his time. Basho's interest in Chinese classics was vitally important to his poetic development; it was indeed Chinese literature that played a crucial role at the moment the poet had to seek his way beyond the Danrin School. Contending that Chinese literature helped open the poet's eye, Akutagawa declares: "At least in Japanese literature light has always come from a western direction. Basho was no exception to this pattern. Just imagine how 'modern' his haiku appeared to his contemporaries." As for the poet's intimacy with his time, he also remarks: "Basho was never a poet who stood aloof. On the contrary, he responded to his time with all his soul." And stressing the fact that he was a poet of the Genroku period which produced Chikamatsu in drama, Saikaku in fiction, and Moronobu in painting, Akutagawa once again drives his point home: "Basho was a poet who felt the spirit of his time most intensely and sang it most boldly since the time of the *Manyoshu*."

The poet's daemonic spirit, his love for common things, his keen ear for music, his magical synaesthesia, his absorption of a foreign literature, and his intimacy with the life around him —these were the points which fascinated Akutagawa as he studied Basho. In Basho he saw his own image. If this is a peculiarity of an artist's criticism, it is also what makes his critical pronouncement so personal, immediate, and perceptive.

The same may be said for "Literary, Too Literary," a series of essays Akutagawa wrote for magazines during the last several months of his life. In the course of 50 chapters (the last ten in the supplement) Akutagawa treats of a variety of topics all related to literary and artistic matters. There are as many artists as there are topics—new and old, Japanese and Western. As we go through this long series we cannot but be impressed with the writer's intelligence, insight, candor, and intensity, and at the same time be reminded that all the while he was writing these chapters he knew they were going to be his critical testament.

"Literary, Too Literary" opens with the Akutagawa-Tanizaki debate over the pure novel, or the novel without the so-called story element. In defense of the pure novel Akutagawa argues that while perhaps no novel can exist without this story element (just as no painting does without *dessin*), it can hardly be considered a primary factor determining the value of a novel. The pure novel, he points out, is a kind of fiction approaching poetry, while remaining closer to fiction than to prose poetry. Not necessarily the best kind of fiction, it is, from the point of view of poetic purity or for its lack of popular interest, beyond doubt the purest. In painting Cézanne comes close to what the pure novel attempts to create; some of its literary examples, says Akutagawa, are the works of the early German naturalists, and above all those of the French writer Jules Renard and the Japanese Shiga Naoya. Appearing somewhat unfinished at first, the pure novel is the product of "an observant eye and a sensitive mind."

Freely disagreeing with Tanizaki's assertion that in literature the novel enjoys maximum architectonic beauty, Akutagawa submits that although structural beauty is never absent in any literary form, the form relying most on such beauty is not fiction but drama. Then he cites *The Tale of Genji* and contemporary examples including Tanizaki's own as the most eloquent counter-proofs to the opponent's stand that the general paucity of this constructive ability is characteristic of the Japanese. In their ability to construct the novel the Japanese in his opinion do not fall behind the Chinese, even though they may not possess the kind of sheer physical strength the Chinese have shown in their long novels. It is not these qualities but poetic spirit that ultimately decides the value of a work of art. Then, concerning his own choice of genres, Akutagawa explains: "I write fiction because it is the most inclusive of all literary genres. Had I been born in the West that has perfected a form of long poetry, I might have become a poet rather than a novelist."

Returning to his initial point, poetic purity, he reiterates that while many factors may contribute toward making a writer representative of his time, it is the purity of his poetic spirit that determines his permanence. In this he finds himself in complete sympathy with Gide's view: To be a great poet means nothing. One has to strive to be a pure poet. The purest of all contemporary Japanese writers is, in Akutagawa's opinion, Shiga Naoya, whom he personally feared as much as he envied. First, Shiga's works seem to him to reveal, among other things, the impress of an artist capable of a good and clean life, a kind of moral purity which is bound to cause a sensitive soul to suffer, and this anguish of a moral soul is central to his masterpiece, *A Dark Night's Journey.* Second, Shiga, says Akutagawa, is a realist who does not depend on fancy or fantasy; and in the realism which permeates his work to the last detail he outdoes even Tolstoy. And third, what makes Shiga's realism unique is his poetic spirit which is deeply entrenched in Oriental tradition, whether or not he himself is conscious of it (here again Akutagawa confesses: "It was ten years ago that I confined all artistic activities within the boundary of consciousness"), and this poetic spirit, coupled with his technical mastery, endows his most prosaic work with a singular beauty.[9]

The poetic spirit, as Akutagawa further explains it, is lyrical in the broadest sense of the term. It manifests itself everywhere in literature, whether in *Madame Bovary, Hamlet, The Divine Comedy,* or *Gulliver's Travels.* Whatever thought, whatever idea, in order to enter into a literary work, must filter through the purifying fire of this poetic spirit, and the degree of this purifying fire at once determines the quality of a given work. Viewed in this light, Ogai falls short of Soseki. Technically, Ogai's poetry leaves nothing to be desired, but, Akutagawa regrets, it lacks "something subtle." The same with his novels and drama, perfectly executed as they are. Here is what separates Ogai from Soseki, whose Chinese poetry, for instance, successfully embodies such subtle lyricism. To Akutagawa this amounts to saying that Ogai is not a poet in the sense that Soseki is. And this same spirit he demands from proletarian literature. It can be genuine literature, "poetry of life," only if it grows out of what he calls the proletarian soul. And to give complete expression to this poetic spirit is what he means by an artist's passion for perfection.

As Akutagawa admits, the poet within himself, to whom all his literary activities are dedicated, responds to many calls —calls of proletarian arts, the Garden of Epicurus, and so forth, but the most irresistible of all is the call of brutality or savage beauty.[10] By this quality he explains the fundamental difference between Renoir and van Gogh, Renoir and Gauguin. While Renoir, like his charming women, is elegance itself, there is something very special about van Gogh's cypresses and suns, a quality of somber intensity that they cast over his canvases. What is it, Akutagawa asks, that makes Gauguin's Tahitian women at once repulsive and fascinating? It is, according to him, the human animal these dark-skinned women represent. The lures of van Gogh's landscape may be different in kind from those of Gauguin's women, but there is one thing common to both painters, he says, something intense that whets our artistic appetite—something in the depth of our soul that is desperately seeking expression.

Still another call that often bestirs Akutagawa is the call

of the West, whose matrix he finds in "mysterious Greece." The best way to feel it, he suggests, is to look at the beauty of those Greek gods which, thoroughly sensuous and sensual, contains something ineffable—what he might call the lure of the supernatural. Akutagawa is surprised to find this "ineffable fragrance of musk" which penetrates marble statues also appearing in Baudelaire and Valéry. While he is aware of both the Hellenistic and Hebraic traditions it is primarily from Greece that he hears the call of the West as opposed to the East. As long as there is the West, this "mysterious Greece," while frustrating all attempts to translate Western masterpieces, will continue to captivate the Oriental soul. There are many views of the West, to be sure, but as Akutagawa states: "Behind these various images of the West there is a phoenix always wide-awake—mysterious Greece. And that is what I am afraid of. Afraid of? Perhaps not. Just the same I cannot but feel something akin to the animal magnetism that draws us, no matter how we may resist."

"Literary, Too Literary" closes with a chapter entitled "The Literary Arctic." Akutagawa suggests that the most literary literature only spellbinds us, rendering our souls static within its own circle of ecstasy—one of the art's terrible charms. From the activist point of view it can be said that art possesses power to emasculate us. This is precisely what Heine complained about in regard to Goethe's art, much as he admired it. Akutagawa wonders if proletarian artists realize that their very weapon may sooner or later render them impotent. "Having made endeavors in my own fashion, I now begin to realize this emasculatory power of art. Even this alone is sufficient to concern me. Indeed, the literary arctic, as Heine said, does not differ from the stone man of antiquity—who, even while smiling, remains cold and immobile as ever."[11]

A significant contrast to this, however, is "Two Western Painters," the last chapter of the Supplement "Literary, Too Literary." It reads:

> Picasso is always storming a castle, a castle such as is vulnerable only to Joan of Arc. Perhaps he knows it is invul-

nerable. But just the same he stubbornly persists in his solitary attack under the rain of missiles. Turn from this Picasso to Matisse. I am sure I am not the only one to feel at home. Matisse is running a yacht on the sea, a world away from the clangor of weapons and the smoke of gun powder. All he sets up in the wind is a peach-colored sail with white stripes. When I happened to come across these two painters' works, I felt sympathy with Picasso and a mixture of intimacy and envy toward Matisse. Matisse's superb realism is at once apparent even to an amateur like me. His realistic training, though adding luster to his canvas, may somewhat disrupt its ornamental effectiveness. Should I have to choose, however, I would take Picasso, the Picasso with his plumes scorched and his lance broken.

Renoir and van Gogh, Renoir and Gauguin, and Matisse and Picasso—these contrasting figures clearly indicate a pattern long familiar to Akutagawa. His alternation between affection and admiration towards these painters is part of that tension between life and art which made his career intensely dramatic. What is significant here is Akutagawa's final preference of van Gogh, Gauguin, and Picasso to Renoir and Matisse.[12] Picasso fighting against enormous odds comes close to echoing the Akutagawa who is attempting something almost humanly impossible—in the face of death.

3

Among the dozen stories Akutagawa wrote during this last period four stand out: "The House of Genkaku," "Kappa," "The Mirage," and "Cogwheels," all of which attest to his unimpaired skill as an artist. Written during the last days of his life, they all reflect his determination to remain an artist to the end, transforming his shattered life into perfected art. Representing each of four types of novel, conventional, allegorical, pure, and confessional, they sufficiently compensate for his deeply felt sense of defeat. Born out of his last explorations, they suggest the possibility that art can ultimately triumph over life, even if the cost be death itself.

"The House of Genkaku" (January 1927) completes his cycle of realistic stories which includes "Oritsu and Her Children," "The Garden," and "A Clod of Soil." Combining the static situation of the first and the tragic spirit of the last two, this story points to the high-water mark of Akutagawa's realism.

Genkaku, once an artist of some fame, has long been dying of consumption. His crippled wife lies in an adjoining room. Attending the old couple in their confinement are the good-natured daughter Osuzu, her well-bred, patient husband Jukichi, and their little son Takeo. Their quiet if not peaceful routine of life is disrupted when Miss Kono moves in to take charge of the patients and Oyoshi, Genkaku's mistress, arrives with her son Buntaro for a brief stay. Osuzu suffers alone when she must step in between Takeo and Buntaro to patch up their apparently innocent fights, and again when her mother, in fits of jealousy, crawls out of her bed.

Miss Kono observes this domestic world with professional detachment; herself a woman of bitter experience, she relishes others' suffering. In the meantime Genkaku's condition is deteriorating rapidly. While Oyoshi is around, he experiences a temporary relief in spite of his wife's undisguised jealousy and the squabbling children. But when Oyoshi is gone, in his terrible loneliness he must face his past crowded with wretched memories. To fight them off he tries to recall the misdeeds of his old friends, but this only casts darker shadows over his own abject life. Then he turns to memories of his innocent early days, but these fade away all too quickly. Even a heavily drugged sleep, his only haven now, offers only temporary peace. Because of the misery that always follows his dreams of Oyoshi and Buntaro, he is now afraid to fall asleep. One day near the year's end he plans to hang himself, and that night he has a frightening nightmare: "Standing amid dense foliage, he peeped through an opening between the *shoji* screens into a room which looked like a teahouse. There he saw a child lying, stark naked with his face turned toward him. The child, though a mere child, was wrinkled all over like an old man." His plan comes to nothing as he is caught in his act by Takeo. Within a week, however, death comes at last, releasing him from the suffering that is his life.

Pity, jealousy, hatred, scorn, resignation, and endurance —all are displayed at the slightest shift in the tense, complicated relationships of these characters who become enmeshed with their own petty egos. There is the quiet suffering of Osuzu caught between her ailing parents and her husband; there is the hopeless tenderness of Oyoshi who must pay her last visit to the dying benefactor; there is the morbid aloofness of Miss Kono who enjoys all this and grins at the clear surface of the mirror every time her help is called for; and above all, there is the lonely despair of Genkaku who in his sheer desperation attempts suicide, something impossible for a man in his condition. Akutagawa records them all with complete detachment. Nothing seems to escape his mirror-like vision. Once projected, the whole domestic scene suddenly turns into a fantastic nightmare world, a sort of living hell. Akutagawa's realism somehow manages to cast a symbolic aura over the house of Genkaku. Speaking of this story, he called it "firm and solid," though the effort was too exhausting.

Although "The House of Genkaku" is now generally considered one of his best stories, indeed the peak of his realism, a panel of reviewers was not unanimously convinced of its excellence and found fault especially with the last section.[13] In this scene describing the funeral a new character suddenly appears, Jukichi's student cousin, deeply absorbed in Liebknecht's *Memoirs*. As the homeward-bound party notices Oyoshi standing forlorn outside the cemetery, they wonder about her uncertain future. The studious cousin has a somber, momentary vision of the fishing village which will be her home, and then returns to his Liebknecht in the renewed sunshine. Some of the panel members felt that this was out of place, whereas others took it to mean something very special, say, the arrival of a new world. Writing to one panel member Akutagawa stated, in effect, that he had to use Liebknecht. "I had an urge," he said,

85

to round up this domestic tragedy in the outside world (hence all but the funeral takes place within the house) and thereby imply the advent of a new era in that world. As you know, Chekhov in *The Cherry Orchard* created a university student to represent the coming generation but let him fall down a staircase. I cannot smile Chekhov's resigned smile at the new era; nor can I have sufficient passion to embrace it. Liebknecht, in his *Memoirs*, heaves a sigh when he relates his meetings with Marx and Engels. Around my university student too, I wanted to cast Liebknecht's shadow.

Then Akutagawa added: "In this I may have failed, of course." This fear, however, was not wholly warranted in view of another panel member who seemed to discern the author's intentions by relating Oyoshi to the matter here: "A sense of compassion common to the low class suddenly shines out of the dark slimy world—like the first light of the dawn. What is suggested here is the arrival of a new friendly world as the old is gone."

In the letter quoted above Akutagawa wrote: "Moreover, it seems to me that life is little joy but much pain, whether you are bourgeois or not." To live is to suffer. Or as he said elsewhere: "Under whatever social condition we cannot always remain in happiness due simply to our being human." It is this tragic sense of being born human that concerns Akutagawa once again in his longest satirical allegory, "Kappa" (completed February 11, 1927).

"Kappa" has been called the author's "last glorious spark" or the "balance sheet of his life."[14] This is largely true as far as it concerns Akutagawa the satirist. He was by now an old hand in the field, having written "Mensura Zoili," "The Monkey-Crab War," "The Strange Island," and "Momotaro." With his sense of wit and irony and his angle of vision, he was an accomplished satirist. There was also his interest in the kappa, a mythical amphibious creature which has haunted Japanese folklore; his interest in this imaginary animal was so long-standing, so personal that one might suspect Akutagawa of seeing his own image in it.[15] Then, there were his favorite satirists and their masterpieces ready to serve him as inspirations: France's *Penguin Island*, Butler's *Erewhon*, and Swift's *Gulliver's Travels*. And finally there was what Akutagawa called his *dégout* with life, a sense of self-disgust which at this time he experienced in abundance. With all these factors helping, Akutagawa wrote rapidly. The result, nearly twice longer than originally intended, was "Kappa," which he called his version of *Reynard the Fox*.

"Kappa" pretends to be an account of the fantastic kappa-land related by inmate No. 23 of a suburban mental asylum. While on his alpine trip the narrator comes upon a kappa and in his subsequent pursuit falls into the subterranean kappaland. Treated for his injury, he is soon made "a citizen under special protection." As he learns the language his circle of acquaintance widens: the physician Chakk, the fisherman Bagg, the college student Rapp, the poet Tokk, the philosopher Magg, the composer Craback, the judge Pepp, the politico Roppe, and many others. In due time he becomes an observant student of the kappa nature, taking mental notes of the way of life in kappaland—its society, culture, and civilization in general, which is in every sense the exact reverse of the human world.

This land of kappa is a sort of topsy-turvydom, as is apparent in the inhabitants' contemptuous attitude toward justice and humanity; their rational approach to family planning; their strange sexual behavior and courtship pattern; their censorship system; their publishing machinery, their effective measures against unemployment, their political structure, their defense programs, their quaint criminal laws, their literary rivalries, their religious cult of the Tree of Life, and their communications with the world of spirits. The narrator does of course admire much of what he sees, though puzzled about certain aspects of kappa civilization. As his initial enthusiasm wanes he finally decides to leave. He returns to human society all right but finds everything human disagreeable. In a moment of nostalgia he attempts to re-join the kappa world but is caught and placed under care as a case of dementia praecox. His only consolation now is to look forward to occasional stealthy visits by his former kappa friends who all convince him that really his doctor, not he, is suffering from dementia.

While working on "Kappa," Akutagawa explained it as something like *Gulliver's Travels*. Indeed, the Swiftean twist is ubiquitous—the narrator reports that in kappaland, as in Yahooland, the female pursues the male, not *vice versa*; that in their publishing scheme the best profit comes from the donkey's brain powder poured into the printing machine, thus securing mass production, reminiscent of some of the experiments at the Academy of Lagado; that as a means of eliminating unemployment they turn the jobless into delectable food, thus solving two problems with one stroke, a faithful execution of Swift's notorious proposal; and that upon return to his own world he loathes the human odor, just as Captain Gulliver does under similar circumstances.

In response to various reviews of "Kappa," Akutagawa wrote: " 'Kappa' grew out of my *dégout* with everything, and above all with myself. All reviewers mention my 'bright wit'— as though conspiring to aggravate my self-disgust." Some of the kappa characters are Akutagawa thinly disguised. There is a delivery-room scene, for instance. The fisherman Bagg addresses himself to his unborn child: "Think twice whether or not you wish to come out in this world." Much to the expectant father's embarrassment, the child replies, "I don't wish to be born. In the first place, I can't stand the mere thought of inheriting your insanity. Moreover, I believe that a kappa existence is awful." So the child's request is granted. (Akutagawa once wrote in "The Maxims of a Midget": "The first act of life's tragedy begins with the parent-child relationship.") There is the ugly-faced philosopher Magg who in loneliness composes "The Maxims of a Fool." Here are some of this lovelorn kappa's words of wisdom: "Pride, lust, suspicion—out of these three, all sins have come for the last three thousand years; and probably, all virtues, too"; "We are not as happy as humans. They are not as advanced as we kappa"; and again, "If we are to adhere to reason, we should deny our existence. The fact that Voltaire, who deified reason, lived a happy life, does prove that human beings are not as advanced as we kappa." And there is the poet Tokk, a devotee of the cult of art for art's sake and practioner of free love, whose tragic suicide marks the climax of "Kappa." In his last note we read a Goethean poem: "And now I shall rise and go/ To the dale beyond this realm of sorrow,/ Where the rocks soar majestically/ And the mountain streams run limpid,/ The dale fragrant with flowering herbs." Looking at his tearful surviving family his friends remark: "One must pity a family that must depend on such a wilful kappa. The fellow apparently gave no thought to what would happen afterwards." The meditative Magg whispers: "To live out our lives, we kappa must believe in some power other than ours." This last confession leads us to the kappa religion dedicated to the Tree of Life, whose motto is: "Live vigorously." Then, the poet's ghost returns at a spiritualist seance, as a voice explains, to find out his posthumous reputation.

All contemporary critics were struck with the novelty of "Kappa" and more or less agreed on its significance in modern Japanese literature. As one critic said:

> Not just a social criticism but also some vague demand—a fantasy pent up within himself—that, I think, was what the author tried to get across. . . . In other words, it seems to be a work meant to portray his own suffering self caught in the conflict between the positive and the passive. In this sense I value its form at least. Perhaps Mr. Akutagawa's intentions were deeper than all this, and striving to get at them he failed to put them in words. In any case I would give credit to his artistic efforts.[16]

The critics all felt that while it was all Akutagawa, "Kappa" failed to grip basic issues; that is, it was a failure as a social and cultural satire.

To Akutagawa, who clearly explained "Kappa" as being born out of his *dégout* with himself, these critics may have appeared to miss the point entirely. They were too close to the work, eagerly identifying everything with Akutagawa rather than viewing it in a larger perspective. The fisherman Bagg, the philosopher Magg, and especially the poet Tokk, often speak for their creator. But this is not all that there is to "Kappa." The modern reader is perhaps in a better position to evaluate its strengths which certainly outweigh its weaknesses. In 1947, when the first English translation of "Kappa" appeared, *Time* for instance featured a full page review under the title "Gulliver in the Kimono" (August 25). Focusing on the philosopher Magg, woman and unemployment problems, the reviewer called Akutagawa a unique satirist in the modern Japanese literary scene suffocating under imperialistic slogans. "Akutagawa's satire," said the reviewer, "seemed almost too good to have been written by a Japanese." This belated tribute of singling him out as a master satirist, insomuch as it came from the tradition of Swift and Butler, would surely please his ghost if it should ever return, as does Tokk's, and surprise his contemporary critics. What is certain now is that "Kappa," though born out of his personal *dégout*, is a work of satire perfectly capable of standing on its own, independent of its creator—beyond its immediate social and cultural context.

When the narrator takes leave of the high priest, he glances back at the cathedral of kappaland: "The great temple projecting its high towers and domed roofs into the overcast sky—like innumerable feelers. There was the eeriness of a mirage hovering over an open desert." While writing this passage, Akutagawa probably had in mind "The Mirage" (completed February 4, 1927), a piece which he had started work on almost concurrently with "Kappa" and which he had just completed. Otherwise, there is nothing in common between the two stories; their contrast once again bespeaks the author's ability to create simultaneously two totally different and antithetical works. "The Mirage" comes very close to being what Akutagawa called a pure story. Of the pure novel, the kind of novel without the so-called story element, Akutagawa stated in his debate with Tanizaki: "I must repeat that I have no intention of writing only this sort of storyless story. We all *can do only what we are capable of*. For one thing, I am not sure whether I have a talent suitable for this kind of stuff. Moreover, to write such a piece is no easy task." Yet when he was through with "The Mirage," he thought it superior to "The House of Genkaku" and "Kappa," and rejected his friends' judgment that it was his "least exciting."

In "The Mirage" there is hardly any story or plot to speak of; instead, there is only a series of incidents and attendant impressions, loosely strung together apparently without any sense of purpose. In this first person story the narrator, accompanied by two friends from Tokyo, goes out to the beach for a glimpse of the much publicized mirage. All they see, however, is the shadow of a flying crow cast inverted over a band of shimmering air. The narrator is more impressed with other trivial things: a pair of black ruts of an ox cart marked diagonally over the sand ("the indelible marks of genius"); a young couple attired in the latest fashion; and a memorial tablet washed ashore belonging no doubt to someone buried at sea. These separate incidents gather gradually and turn into hallucinations as he returns to the beach in the evening; he mistakes a bathing shoe half-buried in sand for a drowned man's foot, a stroller's lighted cigaret for a tie pin, and so on. Trying hard to relate his perplexing dream logically, he blurts out: "It seems to me a lot of things are lurking beyond the threshold of our consciousness." All these clusters of impressions and sensations, as the story moves on, begin to blend into a mirage-like vision.

In this piece Wada Shigejiro noticed the total absence of the author's familiar posture and ascribed it to his alleged loss of critical intelligence, constructive power, and of his sense of humanity.[17] But "The Mirage" is too elusive for such a heavy-handed, clumsy approach. Kume Masao, on the other hand, was more sensitive to its overall atmosphere when he remarked: "Rich in a sense of strange immediacy, rich in a sense of ghostliness, it harbors dark suggestions."[18] Mishima Yukio also hit on the spirit of the story: "A plotless story, it is, I think, the only Akutagawa piece polished to lucid perfection. It always reminds me of Dali's painting—filled with the vast, clear autumn sky, and a driftage of fantastic shape. . . . Things are projected sharply and in their vividness reflect the author's state of mind. A poetic tone pervades the whole."[19] Though seemingly as effortless and transparent as a water-color painting, the story registers every vibration of a subtle mind in consonance with the changing surroundings. All the incidents are carefully selected and arranged in such a manner and order that the story gathers a sense of uneasy suspension which in turn develops into an over-all atmosphere of eeriness with a touch of lyricism. All in all, the story amply demonstrates the author's observant eye and sensitive mind.

"The Mirage" is not the only attempt Akutagawa made to write the pure novel. "The House of Leisure," written a few months earlier, falls under the same category, but as a sort of anti-story it cannot compare with "The Mirage." Although the original working title of "The Mirage" was "Autumn by the Sea," he changed it to the present one, "The Mirage—A Sequel to 'On the Seashore.'" "On the Seashore," written in 1925, is a lyrical reminiscence of a time ten years earlier when late in the summer the then young author stayed with his friend at a coastal village—both fresh out of the university. A passage in "The Mirage" in fact refers to his impressionable youth at the time of seasonal change:

> We stood near the water awhile, watching the gleaming crests of waves. The sea was pitch dark all around. I recalled my sojourn of ten years ago on the Kazusa Shore, and also a particular friend who had stayed with me, who, besides doing his own work, had helped proofread my short story "Yam Gruel."

In many ways "The Mirage" looks back to "On the Seashore." In the earlier story the author noted the butterfly-like beauty of two young girls playing among the waves whose gaiety seemed out of harmony with the hovering loneliness of the late summer beach.

> We were already walking along the windless, deserted water's edge. There was still light—enough to make visible

the footprints of plovers over the vast sandy beach. But the sea at least was dark all over as far as the eye could reach, leaving only a lace of white foam along the curved shoreline.

Comparing the stories we may justly wonder if Akutagawa too was poignantly conscious of the gulf which these eventful ten years had widened. With darkness falling all over the sea, that exquisite sense of loneliness now turns into a sense of eerie hallucination. And if we push further on in this direction, we are bound to come to "Cogwheels."

One of Akutagawa's posthumously published stories, "Cogwheels" (1927) is a first person narrative like "The Mirage." As a confession of the dark night of an agonizing soul, however, it stands a world apart from "The Mirage," not to mention "The House of Genkaku" and "Kappa." In tempting the reader to identify the narrator with his creator in every detail it is unique. This story, which sympathetic friends like Kawabata Yasunari and Hirotsu Kazuo designated as the best of Akutagawa,[20] has a compelling power that even his hostile critics could not but recognize.

The narrator, on his way to the station to board a Toyko-bound train, hears a story about "a ghost in a raincoat" from a fellow passenger. During the trip this strange story haunts him as he encounters all sorts of trivial happenings—a group of school girls returning from their excursion, an old acquaintance back from an overseas assignment, and so forth. Once in Tokyo, he hastens to a hotel when he suddenly notices his long-familiar cogwheels constantly revolving, half-transparent, multiplying gradually. They finally obstruct the vision of his right eye and cause him a severe headache. At the banquet he cannot resist a destructive impulse to defy a well-known scholar seated next to him, and then turning to his dinner he spots a wriggling worm on his meat. After the dinner he walks through a prison-like corridor to his room, and there he discovers a raincoat tossed over the couch. Ill at ease, he brings himself to work on his story, when the telephone rings. He learns that his brother-in-law committed suicide by leaping before an oncoming train; and what's more, at the time of suicide he was in a raincoat!

This first chapter, "Raincoat," sets a pattern for the ensuing four: "Vengeance," "Night," "As Yet?" and "Red Glow." Whenever the narrator tries to resume his writing in the cell-like room, he is frustrated by a series of unaccountable incidents: a missing slipper, a large mouse hiding somewhere in the bathroom, etc. At the same time he is oppressed by gnawing memories of his past glories and infamies, and despairs of books which all seemingly conspire to caricature him and his career. No longer able to bear his loneliness, his regrets and remorse, he runs out and roams the town from bookstore to coffee-house, from cemetery to mental clinic—trying to escape the pursuing Furies. In utter exhaustion he returns to his hotel room for rest hoping he does not come upon a man in a raincoat, but he is tormented first by a dreadful insomnia and then by a drug-induced sleep ridden with foreboding dreams and threatening nightmares. His vision of Icarus' tragic flight always ends in a frightening memory of Orestes hounded by the Furies. During his waking hours he is sometimes cheered by the vision of colors such as rose and green, but there are also ominous colors —red, black and white, which connote darkness and ultimately death. Fearing that he might really go out of his mind, he flees from Tokyo.

The last chapter is appropriately entitled "Airplane." The flight home proves futile. The narrator finds himself helpless once again when he notices a cabdriver's raincoat. One day he goes to the store for a bottle of ink, but all they have is sepia, the kind of ink which always depresses him. On his way out he runs into a Scandinavian resident, Strindberg, who suffers from a persecution complex. Strindberg's black and white tie strikes him as no mere coincidence when on at least four separate occasions he encounters a dog all black on one side. (In Japanese *shi* [four] is a homophone of the word "death.") During a brief visit with his mother-in-law the narrator remarks:

> "This is really a quiet neighborhood, you know."
> "It's better than Tokyo at least."

"Are there many things to worry about here?"
"Surely, there are. It's still part of the world."

That even this resort is part of the world, he readily concedes, being familiar with every crime and tragedy that has happened here in the last year. Then out of nowhere an airplane with yellow wings appears skimming the pine tops and sending a dog and some chickens into flight. He learns that these pilots, being so accustomed to high altitudes, soon cannot stand the heavier air of low altitudes. On his way home he happens to notice some crows perched on a gallows-like swing with one in the middle crowing four times, a bath tub resting exposed on the foundations of a burned-out house, a cyclist with the face of his dead brother-in-law, and a dead mole lying on the road. There again those innumerable cogwheels begin obstructing his vision, followed as usual by a headache. With his eyes closed, he can still see a pair of silver wings folded similar to the trade mark he saw on the radiator cap of his cab. The chapter ends thus:

> Someone hurried up the stairs and suddenly dropped down. As soon as I realized it was my wife, I rose and went into the dimly lit room adjacent to the stairs. There was my wife lying on her face, with her shoulders incessantly quivering—apparently to catch her breath.
> "What's the matter?"
> "Nothing. Nothing really—"
> Finally she raised her face and went on with a forced smile.
> "Nothing is really wrong. I just had the feeling that you were dying."
> It was the most frightening experience of my life—I have no more strength to continue writing this. Living in such a state of mind is indeed a torture beyond description. I wonder if there is someone who would strangle me quietly while I am asleep.

" 'Cogwheels,' " Wada Shigejiro observed, "succeeded only in describing a private, neurotic world rather than the reality of a soul on the verge of death. Fears of one's ruinous fate and the confession of one's sins, despite their apparent excess of self-consciousness, do, however, reveal a streak of truth."[21] Its reluctant praise aside, the statement amounts to saying that "Cogwheels" is a clinical report, and this in turn results from the critic's simplistic identification of the narrator and the author or Akutagawa the man and Akutagawa the artist. Even in detailing the narrator's suffering or the suffering which Akutagawa the man undergoes, Akutagawa never ceases to be an artist, fully aware that unless filtered through art no personal suffering, however tragic, can attain universal and permanent significance. His conscious artistry is discernible in more than one aspect. First, in his chronological compression: The series of hallucinations referred to here, that of revolving cogwheels included, is known to have occurred over a period of time;[22] his brother-in-law's suicide, his writing of "Kappa"—these and other events which crowded the early months of 1927, are for greater artistic effect, compressed into the narrator's brief stay at a Tokyo hotel. Second, his artistry is revealed in his recurring motifs: One series of coincidences and hallucinations—raincoat, cogwheels and headache, worm, slipper, mouse, and colors (red, black and white) moves steadily toward a climax, often vying with another series (rose and green) colors of relief, hope, happiness, dawn, stars, sky, a pair of wings, airplane, and Icarus. If the one symbolizes the pursuing Furies and approaching doom, the other suggests the narrator's desperate struggle for release and freedom. But before the unrelenting agents of life's vengeance his longing for freedom becomes fruitless, as is obvious in the last paragraph of the story. It is thus through an artful interplay of relief and agony, hope and despair that the narrator's suffering becomes intense and convincing. And finally, and most importantly, in this poetic cosmos Akutagawa, by focusing on the last days of his life, recreates a drama of his entire career, a tragic drama whose sole hero is Akutagawa himself.

This sepulchral piece was originally entitled "Tokyo Night," and then "The Night," but Sato Haruo persuaded Akutagawa to adopt the present title. (Partly for this reason Sato ranked it the best of Akutagawa's stories.)[23] The present title is certainly more effective than either of the original titles in its suggestion of the mechanical mercilessness of cogwheels lacerating human nerves. Much like Poe's swinging pendulum, the image has physical impact. Yet both of the original titles are in a way more revealing of the author's intentions: to have the suffering of the narrator represent that of modern man roaming helplessly amidst the ghosts in his dark limbo, his terrifying wasteland. Akutagawa's Tokyo, in this regard, calls for comparison with Kafka's Prague, Eliot's London, and Baudelaire's Paris. The narrator's fear of falling into agonies invisible to the human eye is modern man's fear of Hell, or more properly his fear of falling into Hell.

> Out of the hotel I hurried to my sister's house along the thawed street reflecting the blue sky. The foliage in the wayside park was tinged with black. Every single tree, like a human, had both front and back, which was more frightening than disagreeable. Remembering those souls turned into trees in Dante's *Inferno*, I crossed the streetcar tracks and walked along the row of buildings. Even there I couldn't go on safely more than a hundred yards.

In this passage from the second chapter, "Vengeance," it becomes suddenly clear that what "Cogwheels" attempts to evoke is not a world of fantasies and hallucinations but really a vision of Hell called life as the narrator recalls one of his own aphorisms, "Life is more hellish than Hell itself." The intensity of this vision of life caused one critic to call it the full expression of "eeriness impregnated with a modern sense of morbid anxiety,"[24] and another critic to designate it as "the most profound *fin de siècle* product of Japanese literature" and also remark: "Neither a record of those fantasies and hallucinations preying on a neurotic mind nor an extended episode of modern ghost literature, 'Cogwheels' is almost a mystical account suggesting a fear of something unknown, the most compelling expression of man's lonely soul."[25]

In depicting man's lonely sojourn beset by agonies that often make life "more hellish than Hell itself," "Cogwheels" embodies the themes of two of Akutagawa's earlier stories, "The Solitary Hell" (1916) and "The Wandering Jew" (1917). The first story concerns a Zen priest who claims to have fallen into what he calls Solitary Hell. Unlike other Buddhist hells, it is not underworld but appears suddenly in any place. "In the last couple of years," he confesses,

> I have fallen into this hell. Nothing interests me for long. So I wander from one realm to another, yet unable to escape from this hell. If I cease wandering, then it becomes doubly painful. Consequently I keep wandering as best I can—so as to forget each day's pain. When it gets worse I have no other way but to die. But now. . . .

To this the author appends: "I cannot but feel sympathy with his kind, for in a certain sense I am also one of those victims of Solitary Hell."[26] The other story copiously documents the legend of the Wandering Jew through accounts presented by various alleged witnesses in the course of which the narrator asks two questions concerning the accursed wanderer: Did he ever visit Japan? Why did he alone bear the curse? After many years' search through ancient documents, Western and Eastern, the narrator says he has found what he was seeking. According to the early Japanese Christian mss., the Wandering Jew once set foot in Japan and even met with Francis Xavier. As for the second question, the author refers to a document which quotes the wanderer himself as saying: "In Jerusalem, wide as it was, I was the only one who understood the sin committed against Lord Jesus. Because I understood the sin I was cursed."

    "Cogwheels," whether Akutagawa intended it or not, reflects these two early stories, Buddhist and Christian. Whether one be a Buddhist or not, he is accursed; he is doomed to continuous suffering until that curse is lifted. To the protagonist of "Cogwheels," as to the Zen priest and the Wandering Jew, life is indeed "more hellish than Hell itself," for in Hell there is at least a measure of certainty, though it may mean eternal damnation. The protagonist of "Cogwheels" therefore represents man caught up in the tragedy of being human. Unless he puts an end to his life as the Eastern priest suggests, he, like the Wandering Jew, is fated to roam the earth and await the removal of the curse.

"Cogwheels," with its tragic vision of man, indicates the enormous distance Akutagawa has traveled since 1916, and particularly since his determined descent from the summit of Parnassus. It also indicates that his descent led him not toward the great horizon for which he longed, but instead into his own soul, "the vast African desert of the human soul" which he feared. As he said, art, to be great, must have a window. His window may not open toward the great horizon, but as "Cogwheels" suggests, it does open toward the depth of the human soul, the mysteries of life. Intensely personal, it points to the apex of the confessional novel; at the same time what comes from the voice out of the depths is timeless.

4

Although convinced that art is self-expression, Akutagawa was not so naive as to confuse life with art, fact with truth. As he said in "The Maxims of a Midget": "No one can confess completely; at the same time no one can express anything without confessing." Or as he put it more bluntly: "Unfortunately I know that some truths cannot be told save through lies." This is particularly true when an artist tries to tell truths about himself, because in the very act of confession he must remain an artist. Such was the case with the Yasukichi series, "The Youth of Daidoji Shinsuke," and "Cogwheels," as well as two other pieces which appeared posthumously, "Dialogue in Darkness" and "The Life of a Fool." These last two are manifestly confessional works, but one must keep in mind that they are an artist's confessions.

"Dialogue in Darkness" consists of three parts, in which three voices appear in succession confronting Akutagawa the protagonist. The first voice expresses displeasure at the way Akutagawa has turned out: He is not thorough enough, and indulges in rationalization; he has no thoughts of his own; even if he has, they are full of contradictions; he is arrogant, immoral, and reckless. Fool, scum, egoist, and Satanist that he is, he may still be saved. After this admonishment the voice reveals itself to be that of the angel who wrestled with Jacob at the dawn of the world, and then it vanishes. The second voice, on the other hand, commends Akutagawa's courage: He is human, honest, and suffering; moreover, he is original. It urges him to despise the world and rise above morality; he will be a great one, a superman. Having offered praise and temptation, the second voice also vanishes; it is the voice of Satan who sneaked into Faust's study under the guise of a poodle. Thus, the one calls for repentance and promises the peace of Heaven, while the other flatters his ego and tempts him with glories of Hell. But both are spurned as Akutagawa remains determined to be a poet, an artist.

The third voice, claiming him as his own child, urges him to write unto death. It is a voice familiar to Akutagawa, the one which has deprived him of peace forever. It is the voice of Daemon.

"Congratulate yourself. I do not come to speak to just anyone."

"Yes, I shall beware of your visitation. When you come, there is no peace. Like X-rays, you penetrate everything."

"Then, don't be off your guard in the future."

"I shall not. Only when I am holding my pen—"

"You are requesting that I come when you hold your pen."

"I am not. I am only one of the minor writers, and I want to remain as one. There is no other way to secure peace. But when I hold my pen I may be your captive."

"Then beware. I may take you at your word. One day I shall return. So, 'till we meet—."

At whatever cost he will remain a poet, an artist. This little drama of temptation (we may recall that of Jesus in the wilderness) reveals that at the age of 35 Akutagawa, in spite of himself, re-affirms the paternal claim of his Daemon.

When in the first dialogue the angel remarks: "Maybe, you are a fool," Akutagawa retorts: "That's right. Maybe I am a fool. Books like *The Confession of a Fool* were written by fools like myself." This reference to Strindberg's *Confession* particularly, and more generally to the artist as a sort of fool inexperienced in the way of the world, leads directly to Akutagawa's own, "The Life of a Fool." With little resemblance to the commonly accepted pattern of autobiography or confessions, it presents a series of fifty-one vignettes, each focussing on those most significant moments which marked Akutagawa's life as man and artist.

In an accompanying note addressed to Kume Masao, Akutagawa hopes that in case of publication it will bear no index to the characters who appear and adds that in it he attempts no conscious, deliberate self-justification. There appear familiar names—among others Baudelaire, van Gogh, France, Voltaire, Strindberg, Lenin, Cézanne, Goethe, Villon, Gogol; there also appear memorable events and incidents—those which involved his mother and aunt, Soseki and his death, his marriage, his several love affairs, his friendships, his ailments, his attempted suicides, and the like. Since these fifty-one pieces are arranged more or less chronologically, it is not impossible to identify nearly all characters, places, and incidents. But it would perhaps be better to read "The Life of a Fool" with no concern for fact; indeed it would be more faithful to the author's spirit to read each vignette as a poetic spark, as a symbol, and take the whole series as a string of poetic sparks, as a cluster of symbols.[27] "The Life of a Fool," approached in this manner, will recreate the tragic career of an artist who experienced Heaven and Hell, their joys and agonies.

As Akutagawa himself stated, the man in him perhaps attempted no conscious self-justification; but the artist in him knew full well certain truths would reveal themselves only through art, and that to express these truths about himself he had to rely on symbols. This process of symbolization can be made clear by putting in order "The Youth of Daidoji Shinsuke"

(December 1924), "Recollections" (March 1926-January 1927), and "The Life of a Fool" (June 1927). "Daidoji Shinsuke" comes to a sudden end as the protagonist discovers his soul which defies morality. Despite the author's hope to make the work longer, all he could manage to add were two chapters, "Void" and "Pessimism" (both 1925). Realizing at once that his failure was due, among other factors, to the pace of movement and the form of expression, Akutagawa, in all likelihood, decided to try a different pace and form in "Recollections." In form this second attempt, a series of forty-four brief chapters narrated in the first person, anticipates "The Life of a Fool." The narrative, however, is slow-paced, covering no more than the narrator's early life through his high school years. Furthermore, it suffers from lack of selectivity, many chapters being too trivial, too anecdotal to bear any significant symbolism.

In view of both failures Akutagawa, in "The Life of a Fool," decided to retain the serial form of "Recollections," select only the most significant moments of his life so that the general pace might be quickened, provide each vignette with a symbolic title, and thereby compress his entire career into a rapid, spark-like sequence. As a result "The Life of a Fool," while resuming third person narration, foregoes reference to his early years. For instance, the opening piece, "The Era" (already quoted in the first chapter of this study), by describing him browsing through a bookstore, recreates the era of the *fin de siècle*, the artistic period that nurtured his literary adolescence. For greater effects the author takes advantage of poetic license as in "Sparks," the 36th chapter of "Recollections." One rainy day he is impressed by the sparks which appear when the boots of marching soldiers strike pebbles. This becomes in "The Life of a Fool"—under the same title (No. 8) a crucial moment of his life: With a manuscript in his pocket he watches the sparks issuing from a rain-wet power line. "Still it was discharging brilliant sparks. Life, no matter which way he looked, offered nothing he particularly craved. But those purple sparks, those fiery aerial sparks at least, he wished to clasp at the risk of his life." An incidental observation is here transformed into a vivid symbol of his art. Another example is "A Stuffed Pheasant," the 13th chapter of "Recollections," which concerns his grade school graduation gift. In "The Life of a Fool" it becomes "A Stuffed Swan" (No. 49).

> It was shortly after completing his "The Life of a Fool" that he came across a stuffed swan in a second-hand store. As he thought of his own life he became tearful and derisive. There was before him only lunacy or suicide. As he walked alone through the dusky street he resolved to await the fate which would unhurriedly come and destroy him.

In the same place he calls "The Life of a Fool" his own version of *Poetry and Truth* which is meant to serve as his swan song.

In "The Life of a Fool" Akutagawa finally accomplished what he had failed to do in "The Youth of Daidoji Shinsuke" and "Recollections." Having come to see his life as a symbol of the tragic career of an artist born in the *fin de siècle*, he now could provide the whole series with one powerful theme which is stated explicitly in the next to last vignette, "Captive" (No. 50):

> One of his friends had lost his mind. He had always been fond of this friend, being painfully aware of his loneliness—loneliness under a cheerful mask. He called on this friend a few times after he lost his mind.
>
> "You and I—we are possessed by a daemon, what they call the daemon of the *fin de siècle*," the friend whispered to him.
>
> Then, several days later, on his way to a hot spring the friend was said to have eaten roses. After this friend was sent to hospital he remembered the terracotta bust he had given him before his illness—a bust of the author of *The Inspector General* his friend loved. And recalling that Gogol also died insane, he had to acknowledge some force which had control over them.
>
> While in sheer exhaustion, he happened to come across Radiguet's last word and once more heard the laughter of the gods. The dying Radiguet said: "God's soldiers are coming to arraign me." Much as he yearned to fight off his own

superstition and sentimentality, no struggle of any kind was *physically* possible. The daemon of the *fin de siècle* was no doubt tormenting him. He envied those medieval believers who relied on God for their support. But to believe in God, to believe in God's love was beyond him—even that God Cocteau believed in.

The idea here, that the narrator's whole tragedy lies precisely in his being born a child of Daemon, underlies "The Life of a Fool." From start to finish it is an artist's confessions in which Akutagawa reveals truths about himself.

In the passage quoted above Akutagawa envies medieval believers who could rely on God for their strength, and in the same breath he laments the impossibility of his own belief in God. Faith was perhaps the only road of promise to one who wished to reject insanity and suicide. This at least appears to be the case with Akutagawa. The Bible was the only book to be found lying by his death bed, and a sequence dealing with the life of Jesus entitled "Man of the West" was the very last writing he did at the time of his suicide. One critic called this work the "true expression" of Akutagawa,[28] and another declared: "That Akutagawa, facing death, reached Christ proves the genuineness of his despair."[29]

Although some critics take his interest in the early Japanese Christians as merely his poetic response to the contemporary excitement over this newly found subject, the persistence of his interest, especially in their martyrs, indicates that his was more than an antiquarian's curiosity and a dilettante's exoticism. As is apparent in his early Japanese Christian stories, Akutagawa saw in a martyr's religious ecstasy living proof of man's capacity for self-transcendence. There is a little dramatic piece entitled "Death of a Convert" (1921), which features a Buddhist convert in quest of the Western Land of Salvation. In it Akutagawa pictured a white lily blooming in the dead man's mouth. Masamune Hakucho questioned the author's sincerity and criticized this particular ending as a cheap artistic trick.[30] In reply Akutagawa wondered if even this day we could see that blooming flower. In other words, he wanted to believe in the possibility of such an intense religious passion, and the ending was his gesture of envy and admiration for such human miracles.

In "The Call of the West," the 31st chapter of "Literary, Too Literary," Akutagawa declared the mystery of the West was to be found in eternal Greece. Even there he was not unaware of the Judeo-Christian tradition, the other half of the West. With due recognition of his own ingrained Oriental nihilism, he in fact compared his tradition with that of Westerners who, after much spiritual struggle, returned to their own Catholicism. In March 1926, when a Christian friend presented him with a copy of the Bible, he was grateful and said: "I have just gone through the Sermon on the Mount. Although I had read it many times before, I am struck with meanings which have hitherto escaped me." For what the Sermon on the Mount in particular and the Bible in general meant to Akutagawa at this point, we must turn to "Man of the West."

"Man of the West" was completed on July 10, 1927, and its supplement on July 23, on the eve of the author's suicide. Consisting of fifty-nine chapters altogether (37 in the main and 22 in the supplement), the sequence is impressionistic and laconic in style like "The Life of a Fool." What it reveals throughout is that Akutagawa is not at all interested in Christianity, its theology, or its church. Instead, he concentrates only on Christ, or more properly on Jesus the historical person as he reveals himself in the Gospels. Having at last come to love this Jesus, says Akutagawa in a foreword, he can no longer regard him as a stranger in the street, though such an attitude may invite the ridicule of many Europeans and modern Japanese. As he puts it, we turn to Jesus, "the mirror of all," not for imitation, but because in him every man discovers his own image.

Mary is everywhere, says Akutagawa, not as "the eternal feminine" but as "the eternal protectress"; she is found to some extent in all women and even in all men. Nietzsche's protest, as he sees it, was directed not so much to Jesus as to Mary and what she represents. The Holy Spirit, which also lives in all, animate and inanimate, is not necessarily holy; it is really "the eternal transcendent," what Goethe called Daemon. Neither a devil nor an angel nor God, it often rises and walks beyond good and evil, threatening to possess all Christs. Jesus is one of these Christs possessed by Daemon. The realization that he was not a child of man but a child of the Holy Spirit signaled his second birth, kindled his "journalistic" genius, and ultimately foreshadowed his tragic career.

Jesus, according to Akutagawa, was a born Bohemian and a Bohemian romantic, a fact which John the Baptist, another Christ, failed to understand with all his insight. Emerging from his trans-logical debate with Satan in the wilderness (similar to Jacob's wrestle with the angel), Jesus established himself as an all-time Journalist-Bohemian. And by virtue of his genius he transgressed all those strictures tradition and convention imposed on his time and society, thus producing the Sermon on the Mount, a masterpiece of his youthful passion. Many women loved him and he offered them his poetic love.

Jesus, declares Akutagawa, was something of a communist; he practiced passive resistance; he lived his life faster and more intensely than anyone else; and above all, he was a poet who found "a greater beauty in a lily than in Solomon in all his glory." Convinced that his mission was to teach his way, Jesus loved his followers more than anyone else, much to his mother Mary's despair. But his own teaching he could not practice because it was "a poetic religion full of paradoxes." For God our Lord that was born with us, for this God, for this poetic justice, Jesus fought resolutely, though he knew that he himself was not all "good." Then came the hour of greatest crisis in his career when on the heaven-piercing mountain he confronted Moses and Elijah with his question: How should one live? Only thirty years of age, yet he knew it was time to reckon with his life. "Jesus, too," writes Akutagawa, "could not but feel a sense of nostalgia for the life of the world below. But whether he liked it or not, his way pointed toward the deserted Heaven. The star that announced his birth, or the Holy Spirit that gave him birth would not give him peace."

In despising the way of the world, worldly wisdom, and declaring the final triumph of his cause Jesus, continues Akutagawa, was "one of those super-fools" ever dreaming of the future. The greatest paradox of his career was that despite his profound understanding of his fellow human beings he could not understand himself, namely his own frailty. Once on the cross, he was only "a child of man" when he cried out, "My God, my God, why hast thou forsaken me?" For this hero-worshippers may laugh at him, and those not born of the Holy Spirit may say "We told you so." It is, however, with this pathetic cry that Jesus came all the closer to us, exemplifying the tragic nature of his career.

"Jesus' career was obviously an impassioned one, as impassioned as that of any genius. He was under the control of his father the Holy Spirit, rather than of his mother Mary. Herein lies his tragedy on the cross," writes Akutagawa in Chapter 36, "Jesus' Life."

> Jesus' life, miserable as it was, symbolizes that of every child of the Holy Spirit that has since followed him into the world. (Even Goethe was no exception.) Christianity may some day perish; at least it is constantly changing. But Jesus' life will forever continue to move us. It is a ladder sadly broken off in the ascent from earth to heaven—still aslant amidst the downpour from the murky sky.

There are also many like Jesus in the East, says Akutagawa. The difference between the East and the West is not as clear-cut as the color of our skins. That is why we are moved by Jesus' life. Every Jesus will suffer more or less in the hands of this barbarous, uncivilized life. The same with the man of the East who has longed to return to eternal nature. "The foxes have holes, and the birds of the heaven have nests, but the son hath not where to lay his head"—this saying of Jesus suggests some frightening truth whose meaning he himself was not fully aware of. Unless we turn into foxes or birds we shall find no haven. With this Akutagawa concludes the last chapter entitled "Man of the East."

This image of Jesus, whose thirty-three year career ended

on the cross, singularly resembles that of Akutagawa as he looks back on his own career of thirty-five years. Jesus as a child of Daemon, Jesus as a super-fool, may remind us of Akutagawa as a Daemon-driven poet-fool innocent of the way of the world. Jesus' debate with Satan echoes Akutagawa's own with the three voices in "Dialogue in Darkness." (Note that Jacob's wrestling with the angel appears in both). And the passage, "a ladder sadly broken off in the ascent from earth to heaven—still aslant amidst the downpour from the murky sky," evokes the spirit of the last lines of "Defeat," which concludes "The Life of a Fool": "In that twilight world he had lived from day to day, as it were, resting on a slender sword with the edge broken." In reading his own tragic career into that of Jesus Akutagawa here may seem narcissistic, but the point is that in so doing he attempted to define the nature of his own tragedy. And it was in Jesus that he did at last find the supreme archetype of his career, so that his defeat might not end in a mere defeat; hopefully it would turn out to be a triumph, just as happened with this man of the West.

Of "Man of the West," Sako Junichiro said: "Akutagawa's writing on Christ clearly illustrates how far such a reading of the Bible without supporting faith can depart from its central truth."[31] That such a reaction is wide of the mark is obvious in view of Akutagawa's true intentions. As he stated in the last lines of "Unto Those Who Are Poor," the conclusion of the supplement: "For the cause of supreme journalism Jesus sacrificed everything. Goethe despised him obliquely, just as latter-day Jesuses somewhat envied Goethe. Like those travelers of ancient Emmaus, we shall forever keep seeking Jesus, those of us who will be inspired." Clearly, it was not to accept faith but to justify his own existence that Akutagawa wrote "Man of the West," the last of his works.

5

Those Fiery Purple Sparks

1

𝓘t was before dawn, July 24, 1927 that, with a fatal dose of veronal, Akutagawa took his life. Lying beside him were the Bible and several letters addressed to his family, relatives, and friends. To his wife he left the necessary instructions concerning practical matters which would arise following his death; to his children, some fatherly advice; and to his friends, accounts to explain his decision to commit suicide. In the one to his painter-friend Oana he described his suicide as an attempt to reckon with his life once and for all, and hoped to be forgiven for this first and last act of wilfulness. In another, "A Note to a Certain Old Friend," a sort of open letter, Akutagawa wrote in substance:

> Probably no one who attempts suicide, as Régnier shows in one of his short stories, is fully aware of all of his motives,

which are usually too complex. At least in my case it is prompted by a vague sense of anxiety, a vague sense of anxiety about my own future.

Over the last two years or so I have thought only of death, and with special interest read a remarkable account of the process of death. While the author did this in abstract terms, I will be as concrete as I can, even to the point of sounding inhuman. At this point I am duty-bound to be honest. As for my vague sense of anxiety about my own future, I think I analyzed it all in "The Life of a Fool," except for a social factor, namely the shadow of feudalism cast over my life. This I omitted purposely, not at all certain that I could really clarify the social context in which I lived.

Once deciding on suicide (I do not regard it as a sin, as Westerners do), I worked out the least painful means of carrying it out. Thus I precluded hanging, shooting, leaping, and other manners of suicide for aesthetic and practical reasons. Use of a drug seemed to be perhaps the most satisfactory way. As for place, it had to be my own house, whatever inconvenience to my surviving family. As a sort of springboard I, as Kleist and Racine had done, thought of some company, for instance, a lover or friend, but, having soon grown confident of myself, I decided to go ahead alone. And the last thing I had to weigh was to insure perfect execution without the knowledge of my family. After several months' preparation I have at last become certain of its possibility.

We humans, being human animals, do have an animal fear of death. The so-called vitality is but another name for animal strength. I myself am one of these human animals. And this animal strengh, it seems, has gradually drained out of my system, judging by the fact that I am left with little appetite for food and women. The world I am now in is one of diseased nerves, lucid as ice. Such voluntary death must give us peace, if not happiness. Now that I am ready, I find nature more beautiful than ever, paradoxical as this may sound. I have seen, loved, and understood more than others. In this at least I have a measure of satisfaction, despite all the pain I have thus far had to endure.

In the postscript he added:

Reading a life of Empedocles, I felt how old is this desire to make a god of oneself. This letter, so far as I am con-

scious, never attempts this. On the contrary, I consider myself one of the most common humans. You may recall those
days of twenty years ago when we discussed "Empedocles on
Etna"—under the linden-trees. In those days I was one who
wished to make a god of myself.

In this letter dated merely July 1927, there is nothing im-
pulsive. Everything in it bespeaks the writer's lucid intelligence,
deliberate irony, and customary concern with poetic effect. In
every sense it is an artist's suicide note. Reading it, some admired Akutagawa for remaining an artist to the end, and others
criticized this very ability, or rather his inability to discard his
habitual mask once and for all, laying his agonizing soul stark
naked. For better or for worse, his was an artist's suicide as
perfect as a ritual.

Our real concern, however, is not Akutagawa's attempt to
make his suicide a sort of artistic triumph. It is rather that "vague
sense of anxiety" about his future which he gave as the prime
motive. We regret his apparent failure to analyze it to our satisfaction as much as to his own, though he stated that it was so
vague, so complex, that he decided to leave it at that. Outwardly at least, as his friend Kikuchi pointed out, there was no
conceivable reason for Akutagawa's suicide in view of his enviable talent and fame.[1]

Left only with this "vague sense of anxiety," many have
struggled to disentangle the complexity of his motives. Accord-
ingly there are various theories and speculations, some far-
fetched and some ingenious, based on everything imaginable,
from his personality to his philosophy, from his family to his
time. Depending on their own positions, commentators have
taken this sense of anxiety as Akutagawa's doubts about his own
art and art in general, or as his fear of the increasing social
unrest. No matter how many facts we may gather, we shall not
be any more certain than Akutagawa himself was. All that can
be said with any certainty is that Akutagawa committed suicide
as a result of his failure to resolve the ever-widening discord
between artist and man, and between art and life. His vitality, or

his animal strength, was no longer able to sustain the merciless drive of his daemon. Much as he longed for peace, his daemon would not allow it, and he apparently felt that death alone could accomplish this task of reconciliation. Rather than leave it to the uncertainty of natural death, Akutagawa decided deliberately to hasten the process so that death itself might be made part of his art. His voluntary death was his last act of self-assertion,[2] in his view the only form of retaliation man is capable of against the gods whose misfortune, as he said in "The Maxims of a Midget," was their inability to take their own lives.

Whatever the motives, Akutagawa's suicide is significant in that there was something inevitable about it. If death by suicide is part of both his career and his art, neither his career nor his art can be entirely understood apart from it. This is what makes it unique among several suicides that mark modern Japanese literature. The suicides of Kitamura Tokoku, Arishima Takeo, Makino Shinichi, and Dazai Osamu, for example, were sensational events in their day but are now little more than incidental episodes in literary history.[3] Akutagawa's death not only shocked his contemporaries but still engages us today, indeed to such an extent that one may ascribe much of his fame to his suicide rather than to his art proper.

What, then, did his contemporaries see in his suicide? And what significance did they attach to it? There were of course some like Hasegawa Nyozekan who denied it any artistic or philosophical implications,[4] but theirs was a minority view, and most artists, critics, and intellectuals felt otherwise. Oyama Ikuo, a noted left-wing critic, saw Akutagawa's suicide as a case of an artist's failure to rise above his bourgeois *Weltanschauung*, and discussed his vague sense of anxiety in terms of the death throes of bourgeois art. His suicide reminded this critic of Petronius' in *Quo Vadis* and Spengler's prophecy of doom.[5] On the other hand, Komiya Toyotaka, one of Soseki's close disciples, attributed the suicide to Akutagawa's personal integrity. That is, his romantic aestheticism was shattered and destroyed as his innermost ethical sense asserted itself, casting a sense of guilt around his art. In a way his death seemed to be more compelling than anything he had written.[6]

Understandably, Akutagawa's fellow artists were the most profoundly schocked, especially the younger writers who had looked upon him as one of their living models. Kawabata Yasunari, one of his younger admirers, observed with compassion: "In a word, Akutagawa, dreaming of Goethe's paradise, plunged into Strindberg's hell. His health, his heredity, and his environment—all these contributed to his suicide. But the real cause was his ethical conscience as an intellectual." His death, Kawabata concluded, effected a revision of the common image of Akutagawa as an intelligent, versatile, proud, and ironic devotee of the cult of art for art's sake, "a drastic revision not only of Akutagawa himself but also of his art in general."[7] To these writers his suicide must have meant something very immediate and personal, possibly their own tragedy that might come. Hori Tatsuo, one of his very few literary heirs, in fact declared: "By his death Akutagawa best helped open my eyes."[8]

2

In one of his notes to his wife Akutagawa instructed the future publication of his works to be entrusted to Iwanami Shigeo because he wished to share the same publisher with his beloved Soseki. This particular instruction which was duly carried out, both demonstrates his unabated affection for his mentor and suggests Soseki's significant role in shaping his disciple's career. A classic case of master-disciple relationship, theirs remains one of the most memorable episodes in modern Japanese literature.

In furthering the intellectual tradition in modern Japanese literature Akutagawa owed much to both Ogai and Soseki. That he was a joint child of Ogai and Soseki is a view generally accepted by literary historians.[9] For strictly literary inspirations, however, Akutagawa often turned to Ogai, as is discernible in several of his stories. One cannot adequately discuss his historical fiction, for instance, without referring to Ogai's trail-blazing work in the field. Yet with all his admiration for Ogai's awesome vitality and intelligence, Akutagawa challenged some of his judgments. Moreover, he openly regretted Ogai's paucity of poetic spirit. To him, Ogai was not a poet in the sense that Soseki was.

In more fundamental matters concerning art and life Akutagawa was indebted to Soseki. We have only to recall that his literary career began with the elder novelist's personal blessings. In a word, though he respected Ogai, he loved Soseki. There was, however, a time when the young Akutagawa of 1915, terribly impressed with *War and Peace*, felt that Japanese writers, even Soseki, had a long way to go. Yet, once accepted as a member of the Soseki circle, he was irresistibly drawn to Soseki's magnetic personality. In a letter of 1916 Akutagawa wrote to Soseki: "I hope you will take good care of yourself. Since your Shuzenji crisis [Soseki's critical illness at Shuzenji in the summer of 1910] we all get panicky every time you take to bed. For the sake of our young generation you must stay in good health." His later decision to give up teaching and join the literary staff of the *Osaka Mainichi* to some extent followed the pattern set earlier by Soseki himself when he first decided to devote himself to fiction writing. Akutagawa's Sunday gathering, a weekly gathering of artists at his home, was probably inspired by Soseki's more famous Thursday gathering. At the same time he wrote much about Soseki; besides his two reminiscences, there are throughout his writings countless references and allusions to his mentor. In "The Life of a Fool" he devoted two chapters to describing his earlier acquaintance (No. 10 "Mentor" and No. 11 "Dawn") and another to recreating his shock at the death of Soseki (No. 13 "Mentor's Death"). In "Literary, Too Literary," also, he admired Soseki's genius. Citing Soseki's novels as the product of his fiery genius Akutagawa said: "Everytime I think of him I am even more impressed with his sublime fury; it is beyond compare."

In February 1916, when Soseki wrote the congratulatory

letter on Akutagawa's "The Nose," he was at the zenith of his fame—but had only ten more months to live. The elder novelist advised the young disciple to proceed in his own way, indifferent to the silence of critics. In Akutagawa Soseki apparently saw the hope of the new generation. Soseki's two long letters to Akutagawa indicate how warmly he cherished his discovery and watched over his future. In both letters Soseki repeated his perceptive plea to the young writer: Don't try to push the artist within you; try to push the man within. Contrary to his mentor's wish, Akutagawa turned out to be an impatient Pegasus soaring at once toward the summit of art.[10] If only he had more closely heeded Soseki's advice, or if only Soseki had lived longer to help tame his impatience, there might have been a new Akutagawa, different from what he was. This is no mere wishful fancy in view of the nature of Akutagawa's tragedy, the depth of Soseki's insight, and the strength of their spiritual bond.

Referring to Akutagawa's habitual use of an allegorical frame as symptomatic of modern Japanese literature, Fukuda Tsuneari wrote:

> It was the irony of fate that in trying to escape from such a world of allegory Akutagawa only ended in writing the supreme allegory, that of identifying Christ with himself. But who could, without religious faith, bear the weight of such an allegory? Nay, precisely because he did not have such faith he was unable to go beyond allegory. Thus Akutagawa Ryunosuke typifies the tragedy of the modern Japanese who could find no haven . . . either in Japan or in the West.[11]

The division of the world suggested here signifies the division of man himself, and, as is apparent in several of his stories dealing with the *Doppelgänger* theme, Akutagawa was acutely aware of and also suffered from this inner division.[12] Speaking of the call of the wilderness on one hand and the call of the West on the other, he admitted that he was perhaps not the only modern Japanese artist to experience such a division. While longing for Oriental nothing-ness, he could not resist the lure of the Christian West. He was neither a Goethean superman nor a

Shiga-type human animal, and yet both claimed their place in him. If this division of the self was the root of his tragedy, it also described the tragic condition of the modern Japanese as a whole.

This tragic dilemma, Soseki also found in himself when he declared: "My brain is half-Western and half-Japanese." The tragic predicament of the Meiji intellectual, and more largely of the modern Japanese intellectual caught in the transition of history, in the chaos created by Japan's all-out westernization and modernization is a theme that runs throughout his novels. The so-called Soseki hero, the Japanese Hamlet, one of his major contributions to modern Japanese literature, personified the tragic isolation of modern man, and nowhere was his problem dramatized more eloquently than in his novel *Kojin* (1912–13). In this work the protagonist Ichiro in his desperate attempt to get out of his isolation, sees only three possible exits: faith, suicide, and insanity.[13]

These were also the three alternatives Akutagawa faced at the terminal point of his career. In "The Life of a Fool" he wrote that there was before him only insanity or suicide. Caught between these alternatives Akutagawa was not unaware of a third possibility, faith. In his early Japanese Christian stories, which Kataoka Teppei called the Ave Maria written in Japanese,[14] Akutagawa had sought more than an aesthetics of martyrdom; in them he had tried to convince himself of the possibility as well as the reality of religious passion in the Japanese. Again in "The Life of a Fool" he envied those medieval believers who fortunately had their Christian God for spiritual support. But all to no avail. Unable to believe in God, he could not believe in the Devil, much as he wished and pretended to. He was too much of an Oriental whose tradition rejects such a dualism, yet to return to his own tradition he found himself perhaps too much of a Westerner. All he could see in Christ was an archetype of pure humanity driven by what he called the daemon. This third possibility thus out of the question, he was thrown back to the original alternatives: insanity or suicide. But insanity was too real and immediate for him to yield even to its romantic fascination; after all, he was, as he himself said repeatedly, a son of an insane woman. As "Cogwheels" indicates, Akutagawa dreaded insanity more than anything else, far more than suicide. So there remained the last and only course he could take: suicide. The moment he realized this, as Fukuda pointed out, Akutagawa willed suicide.[15]

Why, then, did this tragedy occur to Akutagawa alone, and not to either Ogai or Soseki, though all three share the same tradition of modern Japanese literature? For one thing, Ogai, through his public career (he was Surgeon General and later, Director of the Imperial Museum), never ceased being a detached observer, and determinedly so, taking writing as his avocation. Even in his career as a novelist he turned from contemporary themes to historical fiction. Nurtured early in the pessimistic tradition of Hartmann and Schopenhauer, he successfully sublimated his inborn detachment into what he called a philosophy of resignation, and this personal philosophy he applied to his art as well as to his life. Something of a samurai fortified with his rural background, he remained a man of the world to the last.

Here again Akutagawa had more in common with Soseki, who was also a native of Tokyo. But the young Soseki's zest for life was astonishing, as is clear in his early resolution: "To live is the sole end of man." And it was not until his fortieth year that he entered on his literary career, a marked contrast to Akutagawa, who, in his unswerving flight toward the summit of Parnassus, bypassed his youth, so to speak. Moreover, Soseki also had his own personal philosophy of *sokuten kyoshi* (conform to heaven and forsake self), which was firmly rooted in the Oriental religious tradition. It is patently apparent in his novel *Kojin* that this was the only possible solution to Ichiro's tragic dilemma. Much like Ogai with his ideal of resignation, Soseki also in his manner strove to achieve his ideal of *sokuten kyoshi* as the ultimate mediator of art and life. There were of course personal factors, such as inborn resources of vitality, which helped Ogai and Soseki pursue their respective careers with such eminent success. As major shapers of an intellectual tradition both Ogai and Soseki were basically artists most typical of the Meiji period, an age of healthy enlightenment in modern Japanese history. Whereas both had to build their own intellectual foundations, Akutagawa, facing no such task,[16] responded directly to the impulses of his soul with his characteristic intensity and transformed them into art. While this is what makes his art unique and inimitable, his determination to attempt all is apparently what led him to his tragic impasse, and few modern Japanese writers have been willing to follow him. Hori Tatsuo, for example, simply rejected the burden. "Although Akutagawa shouldered everything, I, for one, tried to lighten myself as much as I could."[17] There alone at the end of the impasse Akutagawa still continues to pose problems.

3

"He died at the zenith of honor and then was hauled into the nadir of infamy." This graphic statement by Hagiwara Sakutaro accurately summarizes the fate that has befallen Akutagawa.[18] Surveying his early stories Tanabe Moichi ascribed Akutagawa's fame altogether to the contemporary critics' naïveté and concluded that on the whole he was not as good a writer as we were led to believe.[19] Shibukawa Gyo, in a study of Akutagawa's early Japanese Christian stories, found something freakish about his reputation.[20] Even Yoshida Seiichi, acknowledged dean of Akutagawa studies, voiced a more sympathetic but basically similar opinion: As a moralist Akutagawa was mediocre, and as an artist he was certainly not a genius; at best he had talent.[21] And a recent panel of critics and writers moderated by Nakamura Shinichiro, the editor of *Akutagawa Ryunosuke Zenshu*, after evaluating all phases of his career and art in the light of contemporary writing, expressed more or less the same opinion. In his postscript Nakamura, himself sympathetic towards Akutagawa, wrote:

This panel of contemporary writers, quite unexpectedly, arrived at a negative conclusion about Akutagawa. This fact may also be taken to mean that this Taisho writer who died thirty years ago is still regarded by our contemporary writers as one of their own. How many others of his generation could elicit such critical excitement from those of a new generation?[22]

While the panel's conclusion indicates the lowest ebb Akutagawa's reputation has reached since his death, ironically enough, some Western critics have helped turn the critical climate once again in his favor.[23] Credit must go to a small group of translators and enthusiasts who have kept him alive. We have only to recall how warmly the *Time* reviewer, among others, responded when "Kappa" appeared in English. There was also the impressive success of the movie *Rashomon*, and when Kojima's first volume of translation came out, the general critical reaction was instantaneous and electric. In his introduction to the volume Howard Hibbett, calling Akutagawa "the double victim of an unsympathetic society and a split culture," observed:

> The stories have a dazzling and perhaps deceptive sheen. Superficial critics called Akutagawa precious, or decadent, or dismissed him as a fatiguingly clever dilettante. Unprepared for the strength of his later satires, they supposed him to care only for the superb texture of his prose. Translation protects us from the seduction of this style, yet encourages a similar error, since the nuances of Akutagawa's prose are what conveys the essence of his thought. . . . A master of tone, he gave his stories a cool classic surface, colored but never marred by the wit and warmth underlying that perfect glaze. The composure of his style is undisturbed even by vivid accents of the sordid or the bizarre.[24]

Speaking for the general reading public, one reviewer wrote:

> One thing is certain. Akutagawa does not belong to the jade-and-peonies school of oriental writing. In the spare, textured prose of these six short stories he brings us clear-eyed glimpses of human behavior in the extremities of poverty, stupidity, greed, vanity. . . . Few American readers had heard

of Akutagawa (who was a suicide in 1927 at the age of 35) before last year.[25]

Another reviewer declared similarly: "The six stories which it contains need no recommendation except their own merits—which are fresh and striking."[26] This discovery of Akutagawa by Western critics has, in turn, forced many Japanese critics to review him in fresh perspective, finding there something hitherto unsuspected.

The reasons for Akutagawa's sudden rebirth are not difficult to surmise. Many Western readers are surprised, as with "Kappa," to discover something so familiar in the least expected quarters. Those who have long been accustomed to a stereotyped exotic Orientalism suddenly find in Akutagawa a writer haunted by his daemon and intensely tragic in his view of life. Thousands of miles away from Japan, they are in a better position to meet Akutagawa's own demand: Do not look at me. Look at my work. By comparison, the Japanese are less fortunately situated in that their very familiarity with Akutagawa makes it difficult to separate him from his art. Mishima was quite right when he said unfortunate is the writer whose personality rather than his art is still discussed long after his death.[27] This difficulty of distinguishing works from their author is all the greater in Japanese literature due to its peculiar tradition of the *shishosetsu* which tends to emphasize the intimacy between life and art, man and artist.

As the present study has attempted to show, Akutagawa is far more complex than his legend often leads us to believe. Throughout his three-stage career he underwent a significant change, and his works also reflect his developing view of art and life. Because it is based primarily on his early stories, the image of Akutagawa among his Western readers, refreshing as it is, is by no means whole and complete. Although free of this delimited view of Akutagawa, Japanese critics do not fare any better. Because of the many problems Akutagawa's suicide raises, they are constantly tempted to read his life back into his art. When dealing with various stages of his career, they tend to evaluate his works simply in terms of personal preference. Consequently, those who prefer his last period stress his later work at the expense of the earlier; likewise, those who are interested mainly in his middle period often disparage the work of his other periods.[28] This fragmented judgment by personal preference inevitably makes it difficult to see Akutagawa's writing in its totality. Perhaps it is time for us to seize on the recent change in the climate of opinion, and by tracing Akutagawa's career through its varied stages, re-adjust our view to the complex drama of his inner world. Only by a renewed effort to view his life and art in proper perspective can we do justice to Akutagawa.

From the present inquiry it is apparent that Akutagawa has earned his place in modern Japanese literature for several reasons. First, by opposing naturalism he aligned himself with the intellectual tradition of Ogai and Soseki and developed it further. Convinced that literature is primarily a form of intelligence, he both broadened the function of the latter and enriched the quality of the former, thus re-affirming their greater intimacy. Second, by challenging the peculiar Japanese tradition of the *shishosetsu* he helped to foster the great tradition of the European novel in Japan where the novel might otherwise have degenerated into a form of popular entertainment. This he accomplished by virtue of his thorough training in modern Western literatures and also by his firm grasp of the basic relationships between form and content, art and life. Third, by his intelligence, imagination, and passion he demonstrated the artistic possibilities of the short story, and by exploring its dimensions and limits, helped make it part of modern Japanese literature. Finally, through his dedication to his chosen task, he reminded his contemporaries that literature is a very serious and vital part of life, and thereby he affirmed the dignity and worth of artistic pursuit.

Because his art was born out of the very confrontation of East and West, Akutagawa's significant achievement in modern Japanese literature gives him a rightful claim to a niche in world literature as well. Nurtured by the best of both traditions, his work suggests that the continuing interaction of those traditions may yield yet finer fruits. If, as he himself said, Japanese literature is a new fabric whose warp is native and whose woof is Western, it also characterizes the nature of his own art, which is at once Japanese and Western. Viewed in this light, there may be a time when Akutagawa will stand side by side with some of his better-known fellow writers—Poe, Mérimée, Baudelaire, Maupassant, Chekhov, and Kafka.

Akutagawa once said: "I often think—what I have created would have been written by someone, even if I hadn't been born." Perhaps so, though it is doubtful. The best of Akutagawa's work has the indelible mark of his personality and many of his stories will undoubtedly continue to fascinate the reader with their peculiar *frisson nouveau*. "The world is overcrowded with immortal works," wrote Akutagawa. "If a writer can leave ten pieces worth reading thirty years after his death, then, we may call him a master. If he can write five of the same worth, he is still entitled to the Hall of Fame. And, even if only three, he can pass as a writer." Judged by his own standards, Akutagawa is a master. Over half of his some 150 stories are still readable more than thirty years after his death, and unless chance plays one of its unpredictable pranks, most of his best stories will remain. In their own way they are masterpieces with windows open toward various vistas of life, to apply one of his own criteria for distinguishing excellence from mediocrity. To be sure, none of his best stories are very long, but as he warned, "To confuse massiveness with excellence is critical materialism." He was at heart a poet, a pure poet, as he wished to be. Because this is so his stories will continue to send forth their fiery purple sparks, imperishable sparks struck from life that offer their precious glimpse of the human soul.

Notes

The text used for the present study is the latest Iwanami edition, *Akutagawa Ryunosuke Zenshu* (1954–55), prepared by Nakamura Shinichiro. Volume XIX includes, among other things, a chronological sketch of Akutagawa's life, a chronological list of his writings, and a general index. Volume XX entitled *Akutagawa Ryunosuke Annai* is a collection of contemporary reviews, reminiscences, panel discussions, and critical articles. Hereafter this edition will be cited as *Zenshu* with the exception of Volume XX which will be cited as *Annai*.

Also useful are two critical anthologies: Taisho Bungaku Kenkyukai, ed. *Akutagawa Ryunosuke Kenkyu* (Tokyo, 1942) and Fukuda Tsuneari, ed. *Akutagawa Ryunosuke Kenkyu* (Tokyo, 1957). Although there are some overlappings with the *Annai*, all the three collections are recommended to the interested reader. The last two also contain a chronological sketch,

and all provide an extensive bibliography. They will be hereafter cited as *Kenkyu* (A), and *Kenkyu* (B), respectively.

The standard critical biography is Yoshida Seiichi, *Akutagawa Ryunosuke*, Shincho Bunko edition (Tokyo, 1964), which
includes an appended essay "Akutagawa Ryunosuke: His Career and Art."

Throughout this section the titles of Japanese sources, as
far as possible, are given in English.

Chapter 1

For the historical background of modern Japan, see Ian Nish, *A Short
History of Japan* (New York, 1968); Edwin O. Reischauer, *Japan Past and
Present* (New York, 1953); and Richard Storry, *A History of Modern Japan*
(London, 1960). For the general background of Meiji and Taisho literature,
see Hisamatsu Senichi, *et al.*, *Japanese Literary Thought: A Historical
Development* (Tokyo, 1953); Homma Hisao, *A History of Meiji Literature*,
3 vols. (Tokyo, 1935–43); Ito Sei, *A History of Modern Japanese Litera-
ture* (Tokyo, 1958); Donald Keene, *Japanese Literature* (New York, 1955);
John W. Morrison, *Modern Japanese Fiction* (Salt Lake City, 1955); Oka-
zaki Yoshie, *Japanese Literature in the Meiji Era*, tr. V. H. Viglielmo
(Tokyo, 1955); and Yoshida Seiichi, *A History of Meiji and Taisho Literature* (Tokyo, 1956).

1. Mushakoji Saneatsu, quoted in Yoshida Seiichi, *A History*, pp.
   281–82.
2. For the evolution of the *shishosetsu*, see Hisamatsu, *et. al.*, pp. 223–
   89, and Nakamura Shinichiro, "The Fascination of Akutagawa Ryunosuke," *Annai*, pp. 37–51. Interesting in this connection is Ivan
   Morris' introduction to *Modern Japanese Stories* (London, 1961),
   esp. pp. 16–17; 26.
3. Kikuchi Kan: "No one in the future can emulate his lofty culture,
   exquisite taste, and Oriental and Western learning. As an embodiment
   of the ancient tradition and taste of the Orient and the knowledge and
   taste of the Occident he will remain a representative writer of Japan
   at this period of transition" ("Reminiscences about Akutagawa,"
   Annai, p. 126); Tanizaki Junichiro: "His is an agonizing soul gifted
   with lucid intelligence and breath-taking versatility, yet equipped
   with a constitution and temperament least fit to live in this world"
   (quoted in Yoshida Seiichi, *Akutagawa Ryunosuke*, p. 309).
4. This autobiographical piece is discussed in Chapter 3.

Chapter 2

1. For his translations of France, Yeats, Gautier, and Voltaire, see *Zenshu*, VIII 200–70, and for those left unfinished, see *Zenshu*, XV 134–44.

2. The full titles of these collections are *Konjaku Monogatari* and *Ujishui Monogatari*. The former, compiled in the 11th century, contains over a thousand tales in three sections, Indian, Chinese, and Japanese. The latter, a smaller collection of the Kamakura period, includes slightly less than two hundred tales. For the *Konjaku* and its relationship with the *Ujishui*, see S. W. Jones's introductory essay to *Long Ago: Thirty-Seven Tales from the Konjaku Monogatari Collection* (Cambridge, Mass., 1959), and also D. E. Mills's to *A Collection of Tales from Uji: A Study and Translation of Uji Shūi Monogatari* (Cambridge, 1970).

3. See the essays by Eguchi Kiyoshi, Tanaka Jun, and Ishizaka Yohei, all collected in *Annai*, pp. 55–69.

4. Akutagawa's interest in Poe is borne out by the notes for his two lectures, "Poe as a Short Story Writer" and "One Aspect of Poe" (*Zenshu*, XIX, 82–92), and by some of his stories, such as "The Case of a Modern Murder" (1918). See also Toyoda Minoru, "Akutagawa Ryunosuke and Edgar Allan Poe," *Bungaku Kenkyu* (January 1934).

5. See his appended essay to *Akutagawa Ryunosuke*, pp. 279–86.

6. Quoted in Yoshida, *Akutagawa Ryunosuke*, p. 279.

7. "Akutagawa Ryunosuke," *Annai*, pp. 177–78.

8. This tale and another, Akutagawa's partial source, do not appear in Jones's *Long Ago*. For the original tales used for "Rashomon," "The Nose," and "The Hell Screen," see Yuseido's annotated edition, *Akutagawa Ryunosuke*, ed. Yoshida Seiichi (Tokyo, 1963).

9. For an accurate description of corpses Akutagawa is said to have visited the Medical School (Yoshida, *Akutagawa Ryunosuke*, p. 64), and this visit is mentioned in "Cadavers," the ninth chapter of "The Life of a Fool."

10. Wada Shigejiro, *Akutagawa Ryunosuke* (Osaka, 1956), p. 39.

11. Iwakami Junichi, quoted in Yoshida, *Akutagawa Ryunosuke*, p. 63.

12. Quoted in Yoshida, *Akutagawa Ryunosuke*, p. 291. See also Inakaki Tatsuro, "Akutagawa Ryunosuke as a Historical Novelist," *Kenkyu* (A), pp. 155–71. Ogai's view of history is conveniently found in Chikuma Shobo edition, *Mori Ogai: Collected Stories* (Tokyo, 1953).

13. Cf. Shibukawa Gyo: "His exoticism finally ended in no more than an intellectual curiosity" ("Exoticism and Akutagawa," *Kenkyu* [A], p. 253). For a study of this period of Japanese history, see C. R. Boxer, *The Christian Century in Japan 1549–1650* (Berkeley, 1951).

14. In the postscript to this story Akutagawa cited a fictitious source which caused a great sensation among contemporary historians and collectors. See Yoshida, *Akutagawa Ryunosuke*, pp. 123–26.

15. The dramatic treatment of this celebrated vendetta is discussed in Shioya Sakae, *Chûshingura: An Exposition*, 2d ed. (Tokyo, 1956).

16. The movie *Gate of Hell* is based on Kikuchi Kan's version. In this connection it is interesting to read Lafcadio Hearn's in *Glimpses of Unfamiliar Japan* (Boston & New York, 1894), II, 577–78.

17. For the filmscript, see Kurosawa Akira and Hashimoto Shinobu, *Rashomon*, Film Book Series (New York, 1969).

18. The original version in the *Ujishui* reads:

> Once upon a time there was a man called Ryōshu [Yoshihide], a painter of Buddhist subjects. A fire having broken out next door to his house, he ran out into the highway because the wind was blowing in his way. There was in his house a Buddha which someone had ordered. Also his clothes, his garments, his wife and children, etc. were in the house unthought of. Heedless of that, he made it his business simply to run out; and as he stood on the opposite side and looked the fire had already passed on to his house; and he gazed till the smoke and flames were thick, whereupon people came to condole saying: "What a pity." But he disturbed himself not. Though people wondered at him, he looked at the burning of his house, nodding and sometimes laughing, "Oh, what a gain I have made," he said. "Oh how badly I painted it for years!"
>
> Then those who had come to condole him said: "What is this? What a pity it is that you should thus stand here. Are you possessed?" "Why should I be possessed?" said he scornfully laughing and continuing to stand there. "I had for years painted the Holy Fudō's flames badly. As I now look, I have understood that it is thus that fire burns. Ah, this is indeed a gain. Supposing I live having brought this art to perfection, I can have a hundred houses, if only I paint Buddha well" (Basil Hall Chamberlain's translation, quoted in W. H. H. Norman, *Hell Screen and Other Stories*, Tokyo, 1948, p. 8).

The other episode, from the *Kokin chobunshu*, features another painter called Hirotaka, and only its opening passage is relevant to Akutagawa's story: "Hirotaka, in his screen painting of hell, presented a demon from the tower piercing a man with his halberd; and seeing the scene so vivid and real, he said to himself: 'Perhaps my days are numbered.' Indeed not long after he passed away."

19. "Akutagawa Ryunosuke," *Annai*, p. 180.

20. Ishimitsu Shigeru, however, believes that the presence of this ambiguous narrator actually weakens the total effect of the story. See his study of "The Solitary Hell" and "The Hell Screen," *Kenkyu* (A), p. 270. In response to Kojima Masajiro's similar objection, Akutagawa wrote: "There is, I believe, something to be said for 'the explanatory element in the story.' My narration progresses as two lines of explanation intertwine. While the one takes the positive line to which belong many of your examples, the other proceeds negatively, continuously rejecting (actually affirming) the love relationship between the lord and Yoshihide's daughter. Inasmuch as both lines accentuate each other in building up the narration, neither can be taken out of the story" (Letter of June 18, 1918. *Zenshu*, XVI, 257).

21. In a letter of November 20, 1918 Akutagawa also mentions his increasing fascination with the "civilized brutality" of the Chinese, a quality so abundant in such pornographic works as *Chin P'ien Mei* (*Zenshu*, XVI, 273).

22. "Literature of Defeat," *Kenkyu* (B), pp. 148–49.

Chapter 3

1. Hisamatsu, *et. al., op. cit.*, pp. 283–84.

2. "Reminiscences of My Friend Akutagawa," *Kenkyu* (B), pp. 202–03. Included in his book, *My Old Friend Akutagawa Ryunosuke* (Osaka & Tokyo, 1949).

3. This summary of the social background of Taisho literature is based on Yoshida, *A History*, Parts 6 and 7. See also Ito Sei, *A History of Modern Japanese Literature*, Chapter 11.

4. Masamune Hakucho, while calling "Tu Tzuch'un" one of Akutagawa's masterpieces, objects to his "greenhouse dream," a complacent view of humanity (*Annai*, p. 178).

5. His story "The General" (1921) was censored for its anti-war tone and its satirical portrait of General Nogi the national hero who captured Port Arthur. Of three soldiers on a death mission, an old-fashioned samurai type loses his mind, a new type gets killed, and only a dullard survives. Akutagawa's portrait of General Nogi calls for comparison with Soseki's in his novel *Kokoro* (1914). See Edwin McClellan, tr. *Kokoro* (Chicago, 1957). Criticizing Akutagawa's treatment of the general, Mishima Yukio wrote: "The problem is not that General Nogi is our enemy but that he is present within us" (*Kenkyu* [B], pp. 184–85).

6. The difference between this story and another version entitled "The

Era of Meiji" (*Zenshu*, VIII, 140–45) may once again attest to Akuta-gawa's conscious artistry.

7. Sakai Matsuo's study of this story together with "A Clod of Soil" and "The House of Genkaku," *Kenkyu* (A), esp. pp. 275–78.

8. In his notes to a collection of eight Akutagawa stories: "The Hand-kerchief," "Christ in Nanking," "Mensura Zoili," "The General," "The Flatcar," "The Mirage," "Autumn," and "The Ball." *Kenkyu* (B), p. 187.

9. Yoshida, *Akutagawa Ryunosuke*, pp. 157–58.

10. Uno Koji, *Akutagawa Ryunosuke: Reminiscences* (Tokyo, 1953), p. 456. Incidentally Uno is believed to be the friend mentioned in No. 50 ("Captive") of "The Life of a Fool."

11. "Literature of Defeat," *Kenkyu* (B), pp. 133–35.

12. "Mr. Akutagawa as a Writer," *Annai*, p. 184.

13. "'A Clod of Soil' is particularly good. Together with 'The Hell Screen,' this piece represents the zenith of all his works. In the peas-ant woman Otami's life of endurance one can feel the author's mind. Moreover, compared with the works of naturalist writers, this one is better structured with no traces of levity. . . . Several years ago, when back in the country I read the story in the *Shincho*, I was impressed with Akutagawa's ability to handle a contemporary subject realisti-cally—so much so that I at once sent my reaction to the *Bungeishunju* —although almost none of his works since this one has impressed me" (Masamune Hakucho, "Akutagawa Ryunosuke," *Annai*, p. 181).

14. Compare the present version with another of the same title (*Zenshu*, VIII, 181–86).

15. The panel consisted of Tokuda Shusei, Kume Masao, Kikuchi Kan, and three other members (*Annai*, pp. 78–80). See also Araki Tak-ashi's study of the Yasukichi series, *Kenkyu* (A), pp. 233–42.

16. *Annai*, p. 179.

17. See his reminiscences of Akutagawa, *Kenkyu* (B), p. 240.

18. For Kikuchi's series, see his story, "Keikichi's Temptation," in Mat-sumoto Ryozo, ed. & tr., *Japanese Literature, New and Old* (Tokyo, 1961), pp. 1–30.

19. His diary entry of June 18, 1919 indicates that Akutagawa purchased two books by Joyce, along with another two by Conrad (*Zenshu*, II, 196). There is also an unfinished translation of a portion (Chapter 1, Stephen in the studyhall) of *A Portrait of the Artist as a Young Man* ("Dedalus" [c. 1922], *Zenshu*, XV, 143–44).

20. Originally in the *Shincho* for February 1925. *Annai*, pp. 83–85. The panel consisted of Tayama Katai, Kume Masao, Uno Koji, Kubota Mantaro, Akutagawa himself, and three other members. Shiga Naoya

also regretted the incompleteness of "Daidoji," which seemed to him promising. See *Kenkyu* (B), p. 240. *Kenkyu* (A) includes Kurabashi Yaichi's study of this piece (pp. 285–93).

21. Cf. Mishima Yukio: "The idea that haiku can be written anyplace and anytime without one's genius—this, I think, was Akutagawa's happy state when he wrote his early stories. At that stage his despair, his nihilism was merely an artist's dilettantism, but soon it ceased to be such, turning into a sort of physiological despair as his health failed. Now he couldn't handle his material so effortlessly, and began to think that he needed genius, and that, a genius being a drama of personality, such a drama had to derive from his own self. It was because of such an experience that Akutagawa, in his last group of stories, came to eat into himself" (in the panel discussion "Akutagawa Ryunosuke and Modern Writers," *Annai*, p. 262).

Chapter 4

1. *Op. cit.*, p. 412. For the novelist Okamoto Kanoko's similar description of Akutagawa in the spring of 1927, see Yoshida, *Akutagawa Ryunosuke*, p. 220.

2. Explaining that the story had been written on the day before the magazine deadline, Akutagawa was dissatisfied with the portion describing what happens following the protagonist's return home, and he hoped to revise it before it was republished in a volume (letter of September 17, 1925. XVIII, 137).

3. See Kubota Mantaro's study of the piece, *Kenkyu* (A), pp. 312–17.

4. *Kenkyu* (B), p. 240.

5. The friend here is Hirotsu Kazuo, who also said: "When I read the story I had a feeling that he was going to die" (quoted Yoshida, *Akutagawa Ryunosuke*, p. 221).

6. "Akutagawa and His Critical Writings." *Kenkyu* (A), pp. 126–41.

7. "When Hagiwara Sakutaro pointed out that he was no poet, Akutagawa was unusally upset and tearfully protested, 'I am a poet'" (Yoshida, *Akutagawa Ryunosuke*, p. 295).

8. Akutagawa's notes under discussion are availabe in Cid Corman and Kamaike Susumu, trs., "Notes on Bashō," *Origin*, 8 (January 1963), 32–64. See also Nakamura Kusatao, "Akutagawa Ryunosuke as a Haiku Poet," *Kenkyu* (A) pp. 172–96. For Akutagawa's own selection of 77 haiku poems, see *Zenshu*, XIV, 153–58, and for those rejected haiku and other types of poems (*waka* and *shintai-shi*), see the same volume, 159–254. In 1933 Sato Haruo collected Akutagawa's poems in a volume. For general discussions of Basho and Buson in

the evolution of haiku poetry, see R. H. Blyth, *A History of Haiku*, vol. I (Tokyo, 1963) and Harold G. Henderson, *An Introduction to Haiku*, Anchor Books (New York, 1958).

9. See Inoue Yoshio, "Akutagawa Ryunosuke and Shiga Naoya," *Annai*, pp. 191–209. A member of the idealistic White Birch school, Shiga is an intensely personal writer best known for his autobiographical novel *A Dark Night's Journey* (1921–37), which many Japanese critics designate as perhaps the most successful example of the *shishosetsu* genre and indeed a masterpiece representative of their literature. Cf. Ivan Morris: "it is considered by many critics to be the great masterpiece of modern Japanese literature, but few foreign readers would share this view" (*Modern Japanese Stories*, p. 495).

10. Akutagawa used the same term for what he considered the spirit of the *Konjaku* collection, see p. 42.

11. His diary entry of June 14, 1919 reads: "Romain Rolland says that 'where art terminates there reigns—infinite silence' " (*Zenshu*, XI, 194).

12. Akutagawa's frequent reference to Jacob wrestling with the angel suggests that he may have seen a reproduction of Gauguin's painting *Vision after the Sermon* (1888).

Akutagawa's love for van Gogh is especially noteworthy. Referring specifically to him in "Painting," Chapter 7 of "The Life of a Fool," Akutagawa writes: "For the first time I came to understand painting."

Will Petersen called my attention to their singular affinities. Van Gogh's *Wheat Field with Crows* (1890) may remind us of those same black birds which flit into the world of Akutagawa, as in "The Mirage" and "Cogwheels." And also, van Gogh's "Japanese dream" may be said to have culminated in one of his self-portraits, of which he wrote his beloved brother Theo: "I aim at the character of a *bonze* [Oriental monk], as a simple worshipper of the Eternal Buddha. . . . I have made the eyes *slightly* slanting like the Japanese." (Quoted in Robert Wallace, *et al.*, *The World of Van Gogh* [1969], pp. 70–71.) Van Gogh's Buddha here may call for comparison with Akutagawa's Jesus in "Man of the West."

13. Originally in the *Shincho* for March 1927. *Annai*, pp. 94–97. The panel consisted of Kaneko Yobun, Fujimori Seikichi, Aono Suekichi, Nakamura Murao, and five other members. See also Sakai Matsuo's study of this and two other realistic stories, *Kenkyu* (A), pp. 272–84.

14. Uno Koji, *op. cit.*, p. 608; Yoshida, *Akutagawa Ryunosuke*, p. 238.

15. See Akutagawa's own note on the kappa (*Zenshu*, VIII, 172–74). As many of his letters after 1920 indicate (Nos. 600, 603, 612, 617,

641, 718, 792, and 1170), he was fond of drawing and even writing poems about this mythical creature. With good reason the anniversary of his death has been named "the Kappa Memorial Day." For the general description of the creature, see the translators' note to "The Kappa," Kojima and McVittie, trs., *Exotic Japanese Stories* (New York, 1964), p. 209.

16. Ozaki Shiro, one of the panel members reviewing "Kappa" for the *Shincho* (April 1927), *Annai*, pp. 97–101. This panel consisted of Ozaki, Hayashi Fusao, Kataoka Teppei, Yokomitsu Riichi, and four others.

17. *Op. cit.*, p. 144.

18. Originally in the *Shincho* for September 1927. Yoshida, *Akutagawa Ryunosuke*, p. 226.

19. *Kenkyu* (B), p. 186.

20. Uno Koji, *op. cit.*, p. 522.

21. *Op. cit.*, p. 170.

22. In a letter of March 28, 1927, addressed to his poet-psychiatrist friend, Akutagawa wrote: "Lately again a multitude of half-transparent cogwheels revolve, obstructing the vision of my right eye" (*Zenshu*, XVIII, 209).

23. "Akutagawa Ryunosuke: Reminiscences," *Annai*, p. 162.

24. See Asami Fukashi's study of "Cogwheels," *Kenkyu* (A), p. 298.

25. Nakamura Shinichiro, *Akutagawa Ryunosuke* (Tokyo, 1954), pp. 31, 124. Cf. Hori Tatsuo: "The most original or the most personal, if not the greatest, masterpiece of his career" (quoted in Sato Yasumasa, *Modern Japanese Literature and Christianity* [Nishinomiya, 1963], p. 49).

26. The source of "The Solitary Hell" admittedly comes from Akutagawa's maternal great-uncle. For Masamune Hakucho's remarks on its special significance in the author's career, see *Annai*, pp. 172–74, 177–78.

27. In a review of Will Petersen's handsome bilingual edition, *A Fool's Life*, Thomas Fitzsimmons describes its uniqueness thus: "*A Fool's Life* is both novel and autobiography, and neither" (*Saturday Review*, January 9, 1971, p. 33).

28. Kataoka Teppei, *Annai*, p. 190.

29. Sako Junichiro, *The Tragedy of Modern Japanese Literature* (Tokyo, 1957), p. 202. Pointing out that many baptized Japanese writers, such as Shimazaki Toson, Kitamura Tokoku, Masamune Hakucho, Arishima Takeo, and Shiga Naoya, deserted the church soon after they began writing, the author also observes: "The Church (Japanese Protestant) has failed to provide the kind of love which would

nurture literature. Only Akutagawa, at the terminal point of his career, responded to the call of Jesus and wrote about Him, altogether an exceptional case" (p. 233).

30. *Annai*, pp. 175–76. For Akutagawa's reply, see his letter of February 12, 1925 (*Zenshu*, XVIII, 91–92).
31. *Op. cit.*, p. 234. Cf. Miyamoto Kenji: " 'The Life of a Fool,' together with 'Man of the West,' constitutes the focus and conclusion of his literary career. And they will remain a historic monument in the literature of intelligentsia in transition." See *Kenkyu* (B), p. 159.

Chapter 5

1. "Concerning Akutagawa," *Kenkyu* (A), p. 311.
2. Cf. Shiga Naoya: "It seems to me that Akutagawa's death was his last self-assertion." See *Kenkyu* (B), p. 242.
3. Concerning the suicides of these writers, especially Akutagawa, Arishima Takeo, and Dazai Osamu, see Sako Junichiro, *The Tragedy of Modern Japanese Literature*. For the significance of Dazai's suicide in 1948, see also Ito Sei, *op. cit.*, pp. 335–37. To this list we can now add Mishima Yukio, the implications of whose recent suicide are yet to be clarified.
4. "On the Suicide of Mr. Akutagawa Ryunosuke," *Annai*, pp. 110–12.
5. "Mr. Akutagawa Ryunosuke: His Death and Art," *ibid.*, pp. 112–18.
6. "Death of Akutagawa Ryunosuke," *ibid.*, pp. 163–71.
7. Quoted in Aoyanagi Yutaka, "Akutagawa and His Time: The Literary Arctic," *Kenkyu* (A), pp. 77–79. Kawabata also said that in Akutagawa's works "most of today's intellectuals will detect a symbol of their own tragedy" (quoted in Sako Junichiro, *op. cit.*, p. 201).
8. Quoted in Sato Yasumasa, *op. cit.*, p. 54.
9. For a discussion of their relationship, see Hata Ichiro, "Soseki, Ogai, and Ryunosuke," *Meiji-Taisho Bungaku Kenkyu*, No. 6 (1951) (The Soseki issue), pp. 29–42.
10. Soseki's two letters of August 21 and 24, 1916 are addressed to both Akutagawa and his friend Kume Masao, who were then vacationing in a coastal town (see Akutagawa's "On the Seashore"). See *Soseki Zenshu* (Tokyo, 1956–59), XXXI, 216–18, 220–23. Also discussed in my study, *Natsume Soseki* (New York, 1969), pp. 171–72.
11. "Akutagawa Ryunosuke," *Annai*, p. 238.
12. See for example "A Clown" (1914), "Two Letters" (1917), "The Shadow" (1920), and "Mannikin" (Chapter 35 of "The Life of a Fool"). There is also a passage in the fourth section ("As Yet?") of "Cogwheels" which reads: "Standing before the mirror—which I hadn't

done for a long time, I faced my own shadow, a grinning one. As I gazed at this shadow I recalled my double. This second self of mine, which the Germans call *Doppelgänger*, had never appeared before me. However, the wife of Mr. K, who had become an American actor, had seen my double at the Imperial Theater. (I remember how embarrassed I was when she said out of the blue: 'I am sorry I couldn't say hello to you the other day.') And also an amputee-translator, who is no longer among us, had seen my double. Death may be coming to my double, rather than to me. Suppose it was coming to me—I turned my back on the mirror and returned to the window desk."

13. See my introduction to *The Wayfarer* (Detroit, 1967), translation of *Kojin*.
14. *Annai*, p. 184.
15. *Ibid.*, p. 236. For a view that Akutakawa's suicide resulted from the failure of his art to exercise control over life, see Tsuruta Kinya's doctoral dissertation, "Akutagawa Ryunosuke: His Concepts of Life and Art," University of Washington, 1967. On the other hand, a simple medical explanation of his suicide as a case of hereditary schizophrenia is suggested in G. H. Healey's Introduction to *Kappa*, trans. Geoffrey Bownas (London, 1970).
16. See Hata's article mentioned in Note 9, above. Cf. Kawazoe Kunimoto: "Of our three major intellectual writers, Akutagawa drew the worst lot." See his study in connection with Ogai and Soseki, *Kenkyu* (A), p. 117.
17. Quoted in Nakamura Shinichiro, *Akutagawa Ryunosuke*, p. 164. Cf. Yazaki Dan: "That sense of anxiety which drove him to self-destruction has remained still unconquered till this day of the Showa period." See *Kenkyu* (A), p. 102.
18. "A Note on Akutagawa Ryunosuke," *ibid.*, p. 72. Hagiwara's essay is also mentioned in the preface to the present study.
19. "On Akutagawa's Early Works," *ibid.*, pp. 220–32.
20. "Exoticism and Akutagawa," *ibid.*, pp. 243–56.
21. *Akutagawa Ryunosuke*, pp. 300–02.
22. "Akutagawa Ryunosuke and Modern Writers," *Annai*, pp. 251–95. This panel consisted of Mishima Yukio, Noma Hiroshi, and four other members.
23. See Saito Joji, "Akutagawa Seen Through Foreign Eyes," *Annai*, pp. 239–50.
24. "Introduction" to *Rashomon and Other Stories*, Kojima Takashi, tr. (New York, 1952), pp. 11–12.
25. See *NYTBR*, November 30, 1952.

26. See *SR*, March 7, 1953.
27. Mishima Yukio, in the panel discussion "Akutagawa Ryunosuke and Modern Writers," *Annai*, p. 273. Mishima's remarks here are of special interest in view of his own suicide in 1970.
28. For instance, Kawazoe Kunimoto prefers Akutagawa's last period, whereas Yamamoto Kenkichi finds in his middle period the richest flowering of his art. See *Kenkyu* (A), p. 117, and *Kenkyu* (B), p. 133.

Chronology

1892 Born Niihara Ryunosuke, March 1, Tokyo. Following mother's mental derangement, reared by her brother Akutagawa.

1898 Enters Koto Primary School, Tokyo.

1902 Mother dies. Edits a circulating magazine with classmates. Avidly reads contemporary and Edo writers, in addition to classic Chinese novels.

1904 Formally adopted and given family name Akutagawa.

1905 Enters Third Prefectural Middle School, Tokyo. Excels in all academic subjects, especially history and the Chinese classics. Also reads English translations of Ibsen and France.

1910 Enters First Higher School, Tokyo. In the same class with Kikuchi Kan, Kume Masao, Matsuoka Yuzuru, Tsuneto Kiyoshi, and Yamamoto Yuzo.

1911 Reads Baudelaire, Strindberg, Bergson, and Eucken.

1913 Enters Tokyo Imperial University as an English major.

1914 With Kikuchi, Kume, Matsuoka, Yamamoto, and other friends, revives a little magazine, *New Thought* (February–October). Contributes translations of France and Yeats, as well as short stories.

1915 Introduced by a friend to Natsume Soseki (December).

1916 With Kikuchi, Kume, Matsuoka, and others, again revives *New Thought* (February 1916–February 1917). Soseki's praise of his story "The Nose" establishes him as a new talent. Graduates from Tokyo Imperial University with his thesis on William Morris as Poet (July). Starts teaching English at the Naval Engineering College, Yokosuka (December). Death of Soseki (December).

1917 First collection of stories (May). Second collection of stories (November).

1918 Marries Tsukamoto Fumi (February). Signs a contract with the daily *Osaka Mainichi* under which he writes for no other newspapers (February).

1919 Third collection of stories (January). Resigns from the Naval Engineering College and joins the literary staff of the *Osaka Mainichi* (March).

1920 Fourth collection of stories (January). Birth of first son, Hiroshi (March). Goes on lecture tour to the Kyoto-Osaka area with Kikuchi, Kume, and Uno Koji (November).

1921 Fifth collection of stories (March). Visits China (March–July).

1922 First collection of essays (May). *Selected Stories* (August). Birth of second son, Takashi (November). *Heresy* (November). Health begins to fail.

1923 Sixth collection of stories (May). The Great Earthquake (September).

1924 Seventh collection of stories (July). Edits *The Modern Series of English Literature* (July 1924–March 1925). Second collection of essays (September). Health continues to deteriorate.

1925   *Collected Stories*, the first volume of Shinchosha's Contemporary Novels Series (April). Birth of third son, Yasushi (July). Completes a five-volume anthology of modern Japanese literature (October). *A Journey through China* (November).

1926   Moves to Kegenuma, Sagami Bay (April). Third collection of essays (October).

1927   Suicide of brother-in-law Nishikawa (January). Eighth collection of stories (June). Commits suicide July 24. Posthumous publications: "Man of the West" (August–September); "Dialogue in Darkness" (September); "Cogwheels" (October); "The Life of a Fool" (October). The Iwanami edition, *Complete Works*, 8 vols. (November 1927–February 1929). Fourth collection of essays (December).

1928   Collection of fairy tales (June)

1929   Ninth collection of stories (December)

1930   Tenth collection of stories (January)

1931   Fifth collection of essays (July)

1933   Collection of poems, ed. Sato Haruo (March)

1934   Iwanami popular edition, *Collected Works*, 10 vols. (October 1934–August 1935).

1954   New Iwanami edition, *Complete Works*, 20 vols. ed. Nakamura Shinichiro (November 1954–August 1955).

Akutagawa in
English Translation

Akutagawa is one of the most frequently translated Japanese writers, some of his stories being available in several different versions. Given below are only those English translations readily accessible in periodicals, anthologies, and collections. For those in other European languages consult *Japanese Literature in European Languages: A Bibliography*, a list prepared by the Japan P.E.N. Club.

Bell, Eric S., and Ukai, Eiji. *Eminent Authors of Contemporary Japan. One-Act and Short Stories*. 2 vols. Tokyo: Kaitakusha, 1930–31.
"The Story of a Fallen Head" (*Kubi ga Ochita Hanashi*)
"Tu Tsuchun" (*To Shishun*)
"The Spider's Web" (*Kumo no Ito*)
"The Autumn" (*Aki*)
"The Nose" (*Hana*)

Bownas, Geoffrey. *Kappa: A Novel* (*Kappa*). London: Peter Owen, 1970.

Corman, Cid, and Kamaike, Susumu. "Notes on Basho" (*Basho Zakki* and *Zoku Basho Zakki*), *Origin*, 8 (January 1963).

Daniels, F. J. *Japanese Prose*. London: Lund Humphries, 1944.
"The Spiderthread" (*Kumo no Ito*)

Katayama, Tadao. "Man of the West" (*Seiho no Hito*), *The Reeds*, VIII (1962).

Keene, Donald (ed.). *Modern Japanese Literature*. New York: Grove Press, 1956.
"Kesa and Morito" (*Kesa to Morito*) tr. Howard Hibbett
"Hell Screen" (*Jigokuhen*), tr. W. H. H. Norman

Kitajima, Hisao. "Autumn" (*Aki*), adapted by Thomas H. Carter, *Shenandoah* (Winter, 1954).

Kojima, Takashi. *Rashomon and Other Stories*. New York: Liveright, 1952.
"In a Grove" (*Yabu no Naka*)
"Rashomon" (*Rashomon*)
"Yam Gruel" (*Imogayu*)
"The Martyr" (*Hokyonin no Shi*)
"Kesa and Morito" (*Kesa to Morito*)
"The Dragon" (*Tatsu*)

———. *Japanese Short Stories*. New York: Liveright, 1961.
"The Hell Screen" (*Jigokuhen*)
"A Clod of Soil" (*Ikkai no Tsuchi*)
"Nezumi-Kozō" (*Nezumi Kozo Jirokichi*)
"Heichū, the Amorous Genius" (*Koshoku*)
"Genkaku-Sanbō" (*Genkaku Sambo*)
"Otomi's Virginity" (*Otomi no Teiso*)
"The Spider's Thread" (*Kumo no Ito*)
"The Nose" (*Hana*)
"The Tangerines" (*Mikan*)
"The Story of Yonosuke" (*Yonosuke no Hanashi*)

———., and McVittie, John. *Exotic Japanese Stories*. New York: Liveright, 1964.
"The Robbers" (*Chuto*)
"The Dog, Shiro" (*Shiro*)
"The Handkerchief" (*Hankechi*)
"The Dolls" (*Hina*)

"Gratitude" (*Hoonki*)
"The Faith of Wei Shêng" (*Bisei no Shin*)
"The Lady, Roku-no-miya" (*Rokunomiya no Himegimi*)
"The Kappa" (*Kappa*)
"Saigô Takamori" (*Saigo Takamori*)
"The Greeting" (*Ojigi*)
"Withered Fields" (*Kareno Sho*)
"Absorbed in Letters" (*Gesaku Zammai*)
"The Garden" (*Niwa*)
"The Badger" (*Mujina*)
"Heresy" (*Jashumon*)
"A Woman's Body" (*Nyotai*)

Matsumoto, Ryozo. *Japanese Literature, New and Old.* Tokyo: Hokuseido, 1961.
"Lady Kesa and Imperial Guardsman" (*Kesa to Morito*)

McKinnon, Richard N. *The Heart Is Alone: A Selection of Twentieth Century Japanese Short Stories.* Tokyo: Hokuseido, 1957.
"Flatcar" (*Torroko*)
"A Clod of Earth" (*Ikkai no Tsuchi*)

Morris, Ivan. "The Nose" (*Hana*); "The Painting of an Autumn Mountain" (*Shuzanzu*), *Japan Quarterly*, II, No. 4 (October–December 1955).

—— (ed.). *Modern Japanese Stories.* London: Eyre & Spottiswoode, 1961.
"An Autumn Mountain" (*Shuzanzu*)

Nishida, Kazuo. "Otomi's Virtue" (*Otomi no Teiso*), *Asia Scene*, I, No. 2 (1955).

Norman, W. H. H. *Hell Screen and Other Stories.* Tokyo: Hokuseido, 1948.
"Hell Screen" (*Jigokuhen*)
"Jashūmon" (*Jashumon*)
"The General" (*Shogun*)
"Mensura Zoili" (*Mensura Zoili*)

Petersen, Will, with etchings by Tanaka Ryohei. *A Fool's Life.* (*Aru Aho no Issho*). New York: Grossman Publishers, 1970. (Petersen's translation originally appeared in *Caterpillar*, 3 & 4 [April–July 1968].)

Sasaki, Takamasa. *The Three Treasures and Other Stories for Children.* Toyko: Hokuseido, 1944.

"The Three Treasures" (*Mittsu no Takara*)
"Whitie the Dog" (*Shiro*)
"The Spider's Thread" (*Kumo no Ito*)
"Magic" (*Majutsu*)
"The God of Agni" (*Aguni no Kami*)
"Sennin" (*Sennin*)
"Tu Tzu-Chün" (*To Shishun*)

Shaw, Glenn W. *Tales Grotesque and Curious.* Tokyo: Hoku-seido, 1930.
"Tobacco and the Devil" (*Tabako to Akuma*)
"The Nose" (*Hana*)
"The Handkerchief" (*Hankechi*)
"Rashōmon" (*Rashomon*)
"Lice" (*Shirami*)
"The Spider's Thread" (*Kumo no Ito*)
"The Wine Worm" (*Shuchu*)
"The Badger" (*Mujina*)
"The Ball" (*Butokai*)
"The Pipe" (*Kiseru*)
"Mōri Sensei" (*Mori Sensei*)

Shiojiri, Seiichi. *Kappa* (*Kappa*). Osaka: Akitaya, 1947.

Yuasa, T. "The Mandarin Oranges" (*Mikan*), *Contemporary Japan*, VI, No. 4 (March 1938).

Waley, Arthur. "San Sebastian" (*Yuwaku*), *Horizon*, No. 20 (September 1949).

———. *The Real Tripitaka and Other Pieces.* London: George Allen and Unwin, 1952.
"San Sebastian" (*Yuwaku*)

Yu, Beongcheon. "The Cogwheel" (*Haguruma*); "The Mirage" (*Shinkiro*); "The Marshland" (*Numaji*), *Chicago Review*, XVIII, No. 2 (1965).

———. "Dialogue in Darkness" (*Anchu Mondo*), *The East-West Review*, IV, No. 1 (Spring, 1971).

Index

Akutagawa, Ryunosuke: artist stories, 36-42; autobiographical and confessional writings, 3-4, 9, 13-14, 50, 62-69, 92-104; early Japanese Christian stories, 31,32, 53-54, 104, 116; historical tales, 26-36, 53-55; interest in Christianity 31-32, 53-54, 104, 105-8, 115, 116, 131-32; inttrest in the Doppelgänger theme, 115-16, 132-33; interest in the East-West theme, 53-55, 81-82, 97-99, 107, 121-22; literary opinions 11, 12-13, 19-20, 22, 29-31, 43-44, 49-50, 62-63, 75-83, 90-91, 99, 122; literary sources, 21; nursery and fairy tales, 23-26, 51-53; realistic stories, 56-61, 83-84; satirical stories, 52-53, 86-90, 127; suicide and its implications, 109-13, 116-18
  WRITINGS OF:
  "After Death" (Shigo), 73
  "The Aged Susano-ono-mikoto" (Oitaru Susano-ono-mikoto), 31
  "Art, etc." (Geijutsu Sonota), 20
  "Autumn" (Aki), 56, 57-58
  "An Autumn Mountain" (Shuzanzu), 36, 76
  "The Ball" (Butokai), 36, 54
  "A Clod of Soil" (Ikkai no Tsuchi), 58, 60-61, 84
  "Cogwheels" (Haguruma), 28, 74, 75, 93-99, 117, 132-33
  "Creative Frenzy" (Gesaku Zammai), 36-39

"Death of a Convert" (*Ojo Emaki*), 104-5
"Dialogue in Darkness" (*Anchu Mondo*), 72, 99-100, 108
"The Dog and the Flute" (*Inu to Fue*), 51
"The Dolls" (*Hina*), 55
"The Dragon" (*Tatsu*), 17, 21, 45, 46, 55
"The Dream of Lusheng" (*Koryomu*), 17, 21
"The Flatcar" (*Torroko*), 55-56, 60
"The Garden" (*Niwa*), 58-60 84
"The General" (*Shogun*), 127
"The Hell Screen" (*Jigokuhen*), 39-42, 45, 56, 59, 126, 127
"Heresy" (*Jashumon*), 31, 45, 56
"The Holy Idiot" (*Sennin* [1922]), 51
"The Holy Man" (*Sennin* [1915]), 44
"The House of Genkaku" (*Genkaku Sambo*), 58, 74, 84-86, 93
"The House of Leisure" (*Yuyuso*), 92
"In a Grove" (*Yabu no Naka*), 27, 35-36
"Juliano Kichisuke" (*Juriano Kichisuke*), 32
"Kappa" (*Kappa*), 74, 75, 86-90, 93, 119, 120, 130-31
"Kesa and Morito" (*Kesa to Morito*), 34-35
"Lice" (*Shirami*), 17, 21, 46
"The Life of a Fool" (*Aru Aho no Issho*), 3-4, 13-14, 50, 75, 99, 101-4, 105, 108, 110, 114, 116, 125, 130, 131
"The Lilies" (*Yuri*), 55
"Literary, Too Literary" (*Bungeitekina Amarini Bungeitekina*), 75, 79-83, 105, 114
"Lucifer" (*Rushiheru*), 31
"Man of the West" (*Seiho no Hito*), 75, 104-8, 132
"The Marshland" (*Numaji*), 36, 45-46, 55
"The Martyr" (*Hokyonin no Shi*), 32
"The Maxims of a Midget" (*Shuju no Kotoba*), 71, 88, 99, 112
"Mensura Zoili" (*Mensura Zoili*), 36, 53, 86
"The Mirage" (*Shinkiro*), 75, 90-93
"Momotaro" (*Momotaro*), 52-53, 86
"The Monkey-Crab War" (*Sarugani Gassen*), 52, 86
"Mr. Mori" (*Mori Sensei*), 45, 56
"Noroma Puppets" (*Noroma Ningyo*), 36
"The Nose" (*Hana*), 15-17, 21, 27, 28, 46, 61, 115
"A Note to a Certain Friend" (*Aru Kyuyu e Okuru Shuki*), 109-11
"Ogata Ryosai's Memorandum" (*Ogata Ryosai Oboegaki*), 32
"Ogin" (*Ogin*), 54
"The Old Man" (*Ronen*), 15
"One Day of Oishiuchi Kuranosuke" (*Aruhi no Oishiuchi Kuranosuke*), 33-34, 36
"One Day of the Year's End" (*Nemmatsu no Ichijitsu*), 73-74
"On the Road" (*Rojo*), 45, 56-57
"On the Seashore" (*Umi no Hotori*), 36, 92-93
"Oritsu and Her Children" (*Oritsu to Kora to*), 58, 84
"Oshino" (*Oshino*), 54

"Otomi's Virginity" (*Otomi no Teiso*), 54-55

The Puppeteer (*Kairaishi*), third collection of stories, 17

Rashomon (*Rashomon*), first collection of stories, 17

"Rashomon" (*Rashomon*), 15, 17, 21, 27-28, 36

"The Records of the Dead" (*Tenkibo*), 74

"Reflections" (*Tsuioku*), 102-3

"The Robbers" (*Chuto*), 31

"Saigo Takamori" (*Saigo Takamori*), 33

"St. Christopher" (*Kirishitohoro Shoninden*), 31

"The Smile of Gods" (*Kamigami no Bisho*), 54

"The Solitary Hell" (*Kodoku Jigoku*), 98-99, 131

"Spiderthread" (*Kumo no Ito*), 22-26, 27, 51

"The Strange Island" (*Fushigina Shima*), 36, 53, 86

"Susano-ono-mikoto" (*Susano-ono-mikoto*), 31

"The Tangerines" (*Mikan*), 55

"Those Days" (*Anogoro no Jibun no Koto*), 36, 45

"The Three Treasures" (*Mittsu no Takara*), 51-52

"Three Windows" (*Mittsu no Mado*), 74-75

Tobacco and the Devil (*Tabako to Akuma*), second collection of stories, 17, 20, 22

"Tobacco and the Devil" (*Tabako to Akuma*), 31

"Tu Tzuch'un" (*To Shishun*), 45, 51

"The Wandering Jew" (*Samayoeru Yudayajin*), 31, 98-99

"The Wine Worm" (*Shuchu*), 17, 21, 45

"Withered Fields" (*Kareno Sho*), 36, 58

"Yam Gruel" (*Imogayu*), 17, 46, 92

Yasukichi series 62, 63-66, 67, 99; "The Boy" (*Shonen*), 63, 64, 65; "A Certain Love Story" (*Aru Renaishosetsu*), 63; "Cold Weather" (*Samusa*), 63, 64, 65; "The Early Spring" (*Soshun*), 63-64; "The Fishmen's Market" (*Uogashi*), 63, 64; "From Yasukichi's Notebook" (*Yasukichi no Techo kara*), 63, 64, 65; "The Greeting" (*Ojigi*), 63, 65; "The Hack Writer" (*Bunsho*), 63; "The Ten Yen Bill" (*Juen Satsu*), 63; "A Young Mother" (*Ababababa*), 63

"The Youth of Daidoji Shinsuke" (*Daidoji Shinsuke no Hansei*), 9, 62, 63, 66-69, 71, 99, 101-3

"Youths and Death" (*Seinen to Shi*), 15

Arishima, Takeo, 5, 112, 131

Arnold, Matthew, "Empedocles on Etna," 111

Balzac, Honoré de, 6

Baudelaire, Charles, 3, 4, 8, 10, 12, 13, 44, 76, 82, 97, 122

Bergson, Henri, 8, 68

Bierce, Ambrose, 21

Browning, Robert, 21, 35 *The Ring and the Book*, 35

Butler, Samuel, 21, 87, 90; *Erewhon*, 87

Caxton, William, 21

Cézanne, Paul, 77, 101

Chekhov, Anton, 86, 122; *The Cherry Orchard*, 86

Chikamatsu, Monzaemon, 8, 78

Cocteau, Jean, 104
Cubism, 11

Dante, Alighieri, 97; *The Divine Comedy*, 81; *Inferno*, 97
Dazai, Osamu, 112
Defoe, Daniel, 21
Dickens, Charles, 10
Dostoevsky, Feodor, 4, 6, 21, 25, 67; *The Brothers Karamazov*, 25-26; *The House of the Dead*, 67

Eliot, T. S., 22, 97
Engels, Friedrich, 86
Eucken, Rudolf, 8, 68

Fitzsimmons, Thomas, 131
Flaubert, Gustave, 4, 6, 21; *Madame Bovary*, 81
France, Anatole, 8, 15, 21, 30, 44, 52, 87, 101; *Penguin Island*, 87
Fukuda, Tsuneari, 115
Furuya, Tsunatake, 75-76
Futabatei, Shimei, 4
Futurism, 11

Gauguin, Paul, 81, 83, 130; *The Vision after the Sermon*, 130
Gide, André, 80
Goethe, Johann Wolfgang von, 21, 82, 101, 106, 107, 108, 113; *Poetry and Truth*, 103; *Reynard the Fox*, 87
Gogol, Nikolai, 16, 21, 101, 103; *The Inspector General*, 103
Goncourt, the brothers, 4
Goya, Francisco José de, 12

Hagiwara, Sakutaro, 118, 129
Hartmann, Eduard von, 117
Hasekawa, Nyozekan, 112
Huaptmann, Gerhart, 4
Healey, G. H., 133
Heine, Heinrich, 82
Hibbett, Howard, 119

Hirotsu, Kazuo, 93, 129
Hishikawa, Moronobu, 78
Historical fiction, 28-30
Hori, Tatsuo, 21, 113, 118, 131

Ibsen, Henrik, 3, 8
Ihara, Saikaku, 78
Iwanami, Shigeo, 113
Izumi, Kyoka, 8

Joyce, James, 22, 128; *A Portrait of the Artist as a Young Man*, 128

Kafka, Franz, 97, 122
Kant, Immanuel, 68
Kataoka, Teppei, 60, 116
Kawabata, Yasunari, 93, 113, 132
Kikuchi, Kan, 9, 28, 29, 48, 55, 66, 111, 124; "Keikichi" series, 66
Kitamura, Tokoku, 112, 131
Kleist, Heinrich von, 110
Kojiki, 31
Kojima, Masajiro, 127
Kojima, Takashi, 119
Komiya, Toyotaka, 112-13
Konjaku monogatari, 16, 21, 27, 31, 35, 42, 125
Kutoba, Mantaro, 67
Kume, Masao, 6, 8, 9, 62, 63, 67, 91, 101
Kurosawa, Akira, 36; *Rashomon*, 119
Kusunoki, Masashige, 75

Lamettrie, J. O. de, 68
Lenin, V. I., 101
Liebknecht, Wilhelm, 85, 86; *Memoirs*, 85, 86
Literary Era, The, magazine, 48
Loti, Pierre, 21, 36, 54

Makino, Shinichi, 112
Manyoshu, 78
Marx, Karl, 86

Masamune, Hakucho, 25, 39, 51, 61, 64, 104, 127, 128, 131
Matisse, Henri, 10, 83
Matsuo, Basho, 36, 58, 77-79
Matsuoka, Yuzuru, 8, 9
Maupassant, Guy de, 3, 8, 122
Mérimée, Prosper, 21, 30, 31, 122; Carmen, 31
Michelangelo, 12
Mishima, Yukio, 58, 91-92, 120, 127, 129, 133
Miyamoto, Kenji, 42, 59, 131
Mori, Ogai, 4, 5, 6-7, 8, 28, 29, 33, 57, 81, 113-14, 117-18, 121; Youth, 57
Morris, Ivan, 130
Murasaki, Lady, The Tale of Genji, 80
Mushakoji, Saneatsu, 5, 13

Nagai, Kafu, 4, 5; Tales of America, 4; Tales of France, 4
Nakamura, Shinichiro, 118-19
Natsume, Soseki, 5, 6-7, 8, 14, 15-16, 57, 61, 73, 77, 81, 101, 112, 113-15, 116-18, 121, 127; Kojin, 116, 117; Kokoro, 127; Sanshiro, 57
New Fiction, magazine, 16
New Thought, magazine, 9, 10, 12, 15
Nietzsche, Friedrich Wilhelm, 4, 10, 68, 105

Oana, Ryuichi, 59
Osaka Manichi, newspaper, 46, 114
Oyama, Ikuo, 112
Ozaki, Koyo, 8

Petersen, Will, 130
Picasso, Pablo, 11, 82, 83
Poe, Edgar Allan, 12, 13, 20, 21, 68, 97, 122, 125; "The Philosophy of Composition," 20

Racine, Jean, 110

Radiguet, Raymond, 103
Régnier, H. de, 21, 109
Rembrandt, 12
Renard, Jules, 79
Renoir, Pierre Auguste, 44, 81, 83
Rise and Fall of the Minamoto and Taira Clans, The, 34
Rolland, Romain, 12, 130
Rousseau, J. J., 63; Confessions, 63

Saito, Mokichi, 75
Sako, Junichiro, 108, 132
Schopenhauer, Arthur, 68, 117
Seedsman, magazine, 47
Shakespeare, William, 9; Hamlet, 81
Shaw, G. B., 3, 52
Shibukawa, Gyo, 118
Shiga, Naoya, 5, 65, 74, 79, 80, 128-29, 130, 131, 132; A Dark Night's Journey, 80, 130
Shimazaki, Toson, 4, 131; Transgression, 4
Shishosetsu (I-novel), 5-6, 22, 43-44, 62-63, 64, 67, 120, 121
Sienkiewicz, Henryk, Quo Vadis, 112
Spengler, Oswald, 112
Spinoza, Benedict, 68
Strindberg, August, 3, 8, 21, 62, 63, 101, 113; The Confession of a Fool, 62, 63, 101
Swift, Jonathan, 21, 52, 87, 88, 90; Gulliver's Travels, 25, 53, 81, 87, 88
Synge, John Millington, 21

Takizawa, Bakin, 8, 36-9; The Romance of Eight Dogs, 36
Tanabe, Moichi, 118
Tanizaki, Junichiro, 12-13, 79-80, 124
Tayama, Katai, 4, 5, 12; "The Quilt," 4, 5
Time, magazine, 90, 119

147

Tokuda, Shusei, 66, 74; "Toru" series, 66
Tolstoy, Leo, 36, 80; *War and Peace*, 114
Tsubouchi, Shoyo, 4
Tsuneto, Kiyoshi, 8, 10, 46
Tsuruta, Kinya, 133
Turgenev, Ivan, 36

Ujishui monogatari, 16, 21, 63, 125, 126
Uno, Koji, 59, 73, 128

Valéry, Paul, 82
Van Gogh, Vincent, 11, 81, 83, 101, 130; *Wheat Field with Crows*, 130

Verlaine, Paul, 4
Villon, François, 101
Voltaire, 50, 52, 89, 101

Wada, Shigejiro, 91, 95
Watanabe, Kazan, 37-38
Weininger, Otto, 68
White Birch, magazine, 5
Whitman, Walt, 78

Xavier, St. Francis, 98

Yamamoto, Yuzo, 8, 9
Yeats, William Butler, 15
Yosa, Buson, 77, 78
Yoshida, Seiichi, 21, 58, 118

Beongcheon Yu is a Professor of English at Wayne State University. In addition to the present study, he authored *An Ape of Gods: The Art and Thought of Lafcadio Hearn* published by Wayne State University Press (1964).

The manuscript was edited by Carl Fernelius. The book was designed by Richard Kinney. The type face for the text is Linotype Caledonia designed by W. A. Dwiggins in 1937; and the display face is Brush designed by Robert E. Smith in 1942.

The text is printed on Bradford Book paper and the book is bound in Columbia Mills' Fictionette Natural Finish cloth over binders' boards. Manufactured in the United States of America.